True Jihad is the best book I have read explaining Islam to the western mind. Mark has tactfully researched, chosen, and presented the most useful material that a Christian needs to understand Islam and be an effective witness to Muslims. Being a Muslim Background Believer (MBB) myself, I encourage you to read this book and put into practice what you learn.

Dr. Hormoz Shariat, "The Billy Graham of Iran," Iran Alive Ministries

Since 9/11, Islam has continued to appear at the forefront of the news almost on a daily basis. Every Christian who is serious about sharing the greatest news ever to come to humankind, the gospel, needs to familiarize themselves with Islam and how to communicate the gospel effectively with Muslims. In True Jihad, Mark Pfeiffer guides readers through a brief history of Islam, how to communicate the gospel to Muslims, and how to answer their most common objections to the gospel. Highly recommended.

Michael R. Licona, Associate Professor of Theology
Houston Baptist University

Mark Pfeiffer has challenged us to recognize that Abraham's other children are dying of spiritual thirst—and that we are commissioned by Jesus Christ to share Living Water with them. Just as God provided physical water for Hagar and Ishmael in the wilderness, He still offers it to Muslims today. And we are the means of quenching that thirst. *True Jihad* is practical, passionate and provocative. If we let it, it can give us God's own heart for Muslims, a heart of love and compassion; a heart for sharing the Truth that underlines *"true"* jihad.

René Maciel, President
Baptist University of the Américas

We can never learn enough about Islam, but we should also make sure that what we learn is both accurate and relevant. Fortunately, Mark Pfeiffer, no stranger to Islamic culture and beliefs, has written a compact yet helpful introduction to this growing religion in North America. *True Jihad, Winning the Battle for Muslims* offers a history of this 7th century religion that is both succinct, yet thorough. More importantly, his challenge to the reader to build loving relationships with Muslims and thus communicate the gospel in the context of a genuine friendship is a call worth heeding. His answers to the theological objections most often raised by Muslims are practical without ever getting lost in the proverbial weeds of theological apologetics. Well done!

Dr. Rudy Gonzalez, Dean, and Professor of New Testament, Southwestern Baptist Theological Seminary, San Antonio, TX; Former Director, Interfaith Evangelism, North American Mission Board, SBC Alpharetta, GA

"True Jihad" is a must read for all who want a good understanding of the Muslim people and their religion. Mark does an excellent job providing the historical background of the religion and the foundations of the Muslim faith. He gives us insights into the contemporary issues we all face in our dealings with Muslims.

This understanding gives us the foundation to fulfill the commandment given to us by the Lord Jesus Christ to love one another. Mark clearly lays out for us how to strengthen our relationship with Muslims and how to minister the gospel of Jesus Christ to them. He closes the book with insights on theological issues that each of us faces when sharing the gospel with our friends.

This book will strengthen your understanding and your ministry to your Muslim friends and neighbors. And it will make you more effective in reaching out with the gospel of Jesus Christ.

Steve Branson, Senior Pastor
Village Parkway Baptist Church, San Antonio, TX

True Jihad is concise and yet comprehensive, scholarly and yet very practical. I will recommend it to my students.

Dr. Nabeel Jabbour. Professor and Author of the book *The Crescent Through The Eyes of the Cross.*

Mark Pfeiffer has written a very thoughtful book on the responsibility we have as Christians to take the gospel to all peoples, including Muslims. Pfeiffer reminds us that our fears and our ignorance are not acceptable excuses for ignoring the Great Commission and its mandate to reach all nations and people groups.

I especially commend this book as a very readable introduction to the rise of Islam, the early life of Muhammad, and -- what is not often included with introductions to Islam---practical points of theologically sound insight regarding how we can share the gospel of Christ with Muslims, especially in our own cities and neighborhoods. I am happy to commend this work for its clearly stated desire to reach Muslims for Christ.

Dr. Robert B. Sloan, Jr., President, Houston Baptist University

Dr. Pfeiffer's knowledge and heart for Muslims are immediately evident in *True Jihad.* Without the dryness of a textbook, he quickly gives the reader the fascinating basics of the history of Muhammad and Islam, then helps us see behind the veil to the hearts, hopes and worries of the many Muslims living in our communities in America.

Kirk Freeman, Senior Pastor, Crossbridge Community Church, San Antonio, Texas

TRUE JIHAD

Winning the Battle for Muslims

MARK S. PFEIFFER

REDEMPTION
PRESS

Published by Redemption Press, PO Box 427, Enumclaw, WA 98022.

First published by CrossBooks

Printed in the United States of America

This book is printed on acid-free paper.

Any people depicted in stock imagery provided by Thinkstock are models, and such images are being used for illustrative purposes only.

Certain stock imagery © Thinkstock.

Cover photo provided by Photos.com and istockphoto.
Cover idea by David Winter

ISBN: 978-1-63232-800-7

Library of Congress Control Number: 2013904106

TABLE OF CONTENTS

Part Two – Ministering the Gospel to Muslims

Study Guide Available at:

tciis.org

ACKNOWLEDGMENTS

MY SINCERE THANKS TO Glenda Pfeiffer for editing the manuscript, Craig Bird for the author photo, David Winter for the cover design, and Debbie Freeman for all of her advice and help with publicity. I am also grateful to the administration, faculty, staff and students at the Baptist University of the Américas for their endless support for me and The Christian Institute of Islamic Studies.

INTRODUCTION

JESUS COMMANDED HIS FOLLOWERS to "make disciples of all nations." The English word "nations" is translated from the Greek *ethne*, which literally means "ethnic group" or "people group." The command is to make disciples of every people group in the world. The church has failed to obey the Lord's command to disciple Muslims, who in many instances have little or no access to the gospel. Until recently, the church missionary effort ignored Muslims, instead focusing on "the harvest fields" where large numbers of people come to faith readily.

To be sure, some of the reasons why most Muslim people groups are ignorant of the gospel have nothing to do with attitudes of Christians or priorities of mission-sending agencies. Many Muslims live in countries where verbal Christian witness is illegal and harshly punished. Others live in areas difficult for foreigners, whether due to geography, climate or other factors. But none of these reasons constitutes an excuse for our failure to obey the Great Commission as it regards Muslims.

Fortunately, for Christians in the West, Muslims have migrated in large numbers to Western countries. We now realize that Muslims are not strange, exotic people from faraway lands, but are our friends, neighbors, co-workers, and fellow citizens. It seems God has announced, "If you won't go to them, I'll bring them to you." Millions of Muslims now live in European countries and in all the countries of the western hemisphere, including the United States.

To the extent we ever did, we no longer have any excuse for failing to share the good news of Christ's life, message, death and resurrection with Muslims. But even with Muslims living and working all around us, most

Christians remain stoic and uninvolved. Apart from lukewarm spiritual lives, there are other factors at work to keep Christians passive or even paralyzed in terms of witnessing to Muslims. These factors largely revolve around two concepts: fear and ignorance.

This book is designed to address these factors. In "True Jihad: Winning the Battle for Muslims," the author hopes to educate the Christian public on the basics of Islamic history, belief and practice, and address a few of the questions most commonly on the minds of non-Muslims. This is important because to be the most effective disciples of Jesus we can be, we must love others. A large part of loving others is understanding them – their worldview, a bit of their culture, and their view of God and the spirit world. Part one of this book addresses these issues.

In part two, the book provides a simple, step-by-step guide to relationships with Muslims, ministry to Muslims and communicating the gospel to Muslims. One presumption of the book is that there is only one way, Jesus, and his gospel never changes. But there are multiple ways to communicate the gospel and we should tailor the presentation to best impact the recipient. Muslims are no different than other groups in having certain ways of viewing the world. They have specific doctrinal positions and misunderstandings that we must take into account if we wish to *effectively* share the gospel with them. Yet one need not be an expert. Anyone with a little information, equipping and the compassionate heart of Jesus, can be an effective gospel witness to Muslims.

Much of what the book addresses in part two, although written with Muslims in mind, can be translated into use with almost any other group. It should come as no surprise that the most important ingredient for a Christian witness is a passionate love for people. In the end, it is love that compels us to understand people, enter their "world," meet them where they are, and minister to the deepest places of their hearts. May we not only learn about Muslims and learn to minister the gospel to them but renew our love for all people so that all may know him.

PART ONE
ISLAM AND MUSLIMS

CHAPTER 1

The History of Islam

Pre-Islamic Arabia

THE YEMENITE ARMY MARCHED northward toward the city of Mecca. Leading the way was a behemoth – an elephant of enormous size. The goal was the destruction of the House of God, known as the Kabah, at the center of Mecca. The Kabah was the most prominent of many shrines in the western region of Arabia. Pilgrims flocked to it each year, paying tribute to their tribe's particular gods or goddesses. The pilgrim trade provided Mecca a continual stream of income, as pilgrims needed lodging, food, water, and fodder for their flocks. The tribes also came to this commercial center for trade of all sorts.

The Yemenites constructed a magnificent new church, hoping to divert the lucrative pilgrim trade southward. Initially, the Yemenites had been unsuccessful in persuading the tribes of the region to switch their allegiance and worship to the new site. But their peaceful efforts at persuasion fell to the wayside when a man from Mecca, threatened by the possible loss of trade to his hometown, snuck into the magnificent church and urinated inside it. Infuriated, the Christian king set out northward to destroy the Kabah.

The army was formidable. Its success was all but certain. Several times, armies were amassed to defend Mecca and the Kabah, but each time these defenders were routed. Yet God intervened to protect his house. He sent

3

a flock of birds high over the army, carrying small pebbles in their beaks and claws. At God's command, the birds dropped their pebbles upon the army, completely destroying it. The pebbles hit the soldiers in their heads, passed through them and came out the other end. Limbs were torn from bodies. The elephant became frightened and refused to continue. This miraculous event occurred during what became known as the "Year of the Elephant." The events are memorialized in the Qur'an, the holy book of Islam, as follows -

> Do you [Prophet] not see how your Lord dealt with the army of the elephant? Did He not utterly confound their plans? He sent ranks of birds against them, pelting them with pellets of hard-baked clay: He made them [like] cropped stubble.[1]

Modern commentators on the Qur'an attribute this "destruction" of the army to an outbreak of smallpox or measles that struck Mecca that year. Regardless, the event is memorable to Muslims because, in this year, around 570 AD, a baby boy was born in Mecca. His birth was without fanfare. There were no miraculous events, no prophecies fulfilled, and no angelic appearances. The circumstances of his birth were completely unremarkable. His mother named him Muhammad ibn 'Abd Allah.

The society into which Muhammad was born was backward and primitive. Society was organized around tribes and clans within those tribes. Tribes were formed from extended families. Sometimes smaller and weaker tribes would join themselves to larger and more powerful tribes, and sometimes larger tribes would divide. Tribes were constantly at war with each other, whether to obtain food, livestock, grazing lands or women. Every male member of a tribe was expected to fight for the tribe, and the tribe was always there to protect every member. "One for all and all for one" was never truer than with these tribes.

Without government, police, or military, membership in a tribe was the only means of safety and survival. There was no moral or ethic that served to control human passion. The law of retaliation, *lex talionis*, or "an eye for

---

1   Qur'an sura 105, verses 1-5 (cited 105:1-5, and so throughout). All citations to the Qur'an are from *The Qur'an*, M.A.S. Abdel Haleem translation (Oxford: Oxford University Press, 2004), unless otherwise noted.

an eye" was the law of the land, and the only force that restrained human lusts. An attack on a member of one tribe guaranteed a commensurate attack on the offender's tribe. Nevertheless, raiding other tribes, as well as caravans or any vulnerable target, was a way of life for the nomadic tribes of Arabia.

Each tribe had its own god, gods or goddesses, although each may have recognized one supreme god. The Meccan tribes recognized one supreme god, Al-lah, but also worshipped subsidiary gods and goddesses. These included the three female daughters of Allah who went by the names Manat, al-Lat, and al-Uzza. The tribes made pilgrimages to shrines honoring each of these gods, the Kabah being the largest and most prominent of these. Given the war-like nature of tribal society, custom provided for several months per year when fighting was strictly prohibited. Thereby, people could travel in safety to make their pilgrimages. Fighting within the confines of a shrine was also prohibited, which allowed vendors to safely conduct business year around. The Kabah created the context for a thriving commercial environment.

Although highly pagan and polytheistic, the Arabs were familiar with various monotheistic peoples. Tribes of Jews lived in the area. These Jews were probably sectarian, recognizing only the Torah and the Psalms as their scripture because when the Qur'an mentions the holy books of the Jews, it only mentions these books. The Arabs knew the Ebionites, a Christian sect with a presence in Mecca itself. Arab monotheists were known as *Hanifs* who were thought to be related to the Jews and Christians as descendants of Abraham.

In addition to the pilgrimage trade, Meccans were also skilled traders. Caravans carrying trade goods traveled south to Yemen, northwest to the region of Syria and Jordan, and northeast to Iraq. The Meccans and others paid pre-arranged protection fees to pass through various territories controlled by the local tribes. These payments were cheaper than carrying along a force of fighting men sufficient in strength to protect the caravans from raids. These arrangements resulted in alliances among the Meccans and various tribes of the area.

The Arab people were generally uneducated and highly superstitious. Yet those who worked the caravans were familiar with more advanced civilizations. The Byzantines to the northwest and the Persians to the northeast controlled the territories to which the Meccan caravans traveled, meaning the Arabs were exposed to the cultures and religions of these empires. In fact, since caravans were particularly vulnerable at night, traders from throughout the region spent the nights at caravanserais. They gathered around campfires and traded stories of their homelands, people, folklore, prophets and religions.

Although generally uneducated, the Arabs enjoyed the arts, especially poetry. They used poetry to extol the virtues of their ancestors, ridicule their enemies, and express to the public whatever messages they desired. Gifted poets were said to be *majnun*, either possessed by or aided by spiritual beings known as *jinn* (from which we get the English word "genie"). Poets would pin their works to the outer walls of buildings, including the Kabah.

Muhammad's Early Life

Muhammad's upbringing was unfortunate. Before he was born, his father died while working on a caravan. When he was only a few years old his mother Aminah died. Muhammad was shuffled off to a grandfather and then to an uncle, Abu Talib, who ultimately reared him. Abu Talib was the clan leader for the Banu Hashim clan of the Quraysh tribe of Mecca.

Muhammad worked the caravans as his father had done. He was able to travel and interact with those from other lands, cultures, and religions. In addition to various Christian and Jewish groups, he also encountered Zoroastrians from the Persian Empire. Muhammad became troubled by the more advanced and civilized state of these monotheistic religions and peoples compared to the backward polytheism and superstition of his Arab brethren. These foreigners told many stories of prophets and their exploits, often in slightly corrupted form relative to the accounts recorded in the various holy books. But Muhammad undoubtedly noted the Arabs had not a single prophet, nor a holy book, and thus suffered from pervasive superstition and polytheism.

In his work on the caravans, Muhammad developed a reputation for honesty and trustworthiness. He caught the eye of a wealthy widow, Khadijah, who had inherited a caravan business from her late husband. She hired Muhammad to lead her caravans. Eventually, when Muhammad was twenty-five years old and Khadijah was forty, they married. Khadijah's cousin Waraqa bin Nawfal, the Ebionite Christian priest of Mecca,[2] performed the ceremony.

Khadijah's wealth meant Muhammad was freed from the requirements of labor. He often retreated to a cave outside Mecca to pray and contemplate the societal problems he had observed among Arabs relative to the more advanced monotheistic societies he had encountered on his caravan trips. He sometimes spent days at a time in the cave. His fervent prayer finally paid off.

The First Revelation

One day while Muhammad was meditating in the cave, a spiritual being appeared to him a very strange way. The being pressed him against the ground, squeezing his chest so hard that Muhammad thought he would die. The being released the pressure and ordered him to "read." Muhammad replied, "What shall I read?" The being again pressed him to the point of death, released him, and ordered him to "read." Muhammad replied as he had the first time, and then the sequence repeated again. After this third time, upon releasing him, the being ordered Muhammad as follows -

> Read! In the name of your Lord who created: He created man from a clinging form. Read! Your Lord is the Most Bountiful One who taught by [means of] the pen, who taught man what he did not know. (96:1-5)

Muhammad recounts that he recited these words, and the being left him. He was terrified, believing he was possessed by the *jinn,* or had gone mad. He feared what the Meccans would say of him. He determined that he would commit suicide, throwing himself off a mountain cliff. However, the being intervened, assuring him he had been chosen as the Messenger

---

2   The Ebionites were a heretical sect of Christianity, and accepted only *The Gospel According to the Hebrews* as their scripture, rejecting the canonical gospels and the works of Paul. The early church universally condemned this gospel. It is lost to us now but is quoted by the early church fathers. It taught that Mary was the Holy Spirit (cf. Qur'an 5:116) and that Jesus was never crucified (cf. Qur'an 4:157). For an analysis of the Ebionites, *The Gospel According to the Hebrews*, Waraqa bin Nawfal and his influence on Muhammad and the Qur'an, see Joseph Azzi, *The Priest and the Prophet* (Los Angeles: The Pen Publishers, 2005).

of God for the Arab peoples. Muhammad relented but was still distraught. He returned home and told Khadijah to cover him. When he returned to his senses, he explained to Khadijah what had happened. She assured him he was a righteous man, and Allah would not dishonor him. Still unsure, Muhammad and Khadijah went to visit Waraqa bin Nawfal, her cousin, and the Ebionite Christian priest of Mecca. Waraqa identified the spiritual being as an angel of Allah, the same spirit that appeared to Moses. Much later, Muslim scholars came to view the being as the angel Gabriel. Gradually, Muhammad accepted that rather than being insane or possessed by the *jinn*, he was Allah's messenger to the Arab people.[3]

The Meccan Period

For a period of time, Muhammad only shared his experiences with his family, who were the first to accept him as a prophet, and accept the divine nature of his message. But eventually, Gabriel ordered Muhammad to begin delivering the revealed messages to the people of Mecca.

During these initial stages, the message revealed by Gabriel to Muhammad, and delivered by Muhammad to the Meccans, was unobjectionable. Muhammad emphasized the unity of God, moral behavior, and regard for the poor, the widow, and the orphan. He taught that he was a messenger in the lineage of Abraham, Moses, and others in the monotheistic faith of the Jews and Christians. He attempted to attract people by reciting revelations containing familiar stories about these prophets and other biblical stories. He taught that Jews and Christians who followed their religions faithfully would find favor with Allah in the

---

3   Waraqa was highly influential in Muhammad's mission. When Waraqa died, the revelations Muhammad received mysteriously ceased for some period of time. See *Sahih al-Bukhari*, book 1, *hadith* 3; book 60, *hadith* 478; book 87, *hadith* 111 (cited 1:3, 60:478, and 87:111 hereafter).

afterlife. He taught that religion was a matter of free choice, and no one could be compelled to believe anything against their will.[4]

Other than his family, few believed him. His message was unattractive to the Meccans. Strict monotheism meant the Arabian pantheon did not exist. If the gods and goddesses of the tribes did not exist, there would be no need to make the pilgrimage to the Kabah. Without the pilgrimage, the business interests of the Meccans would be severely compromised. However, with the protection of his uncle and clan leader Abu Talib, he met little opposition.

Muhammad began preaching strict monotheism and that Allah only loves those who believe in him alone. It was at this point that resistance to Muhammad began to grow. He also taught that Allah hates all polytheists, whose destiny was the hellfire. The Meccans heard the obvious implication that their ancestors, whose righteousness, bravery, and honor they venerated in their lore and poetry, were all in hell. This message was intolerable. Further, the Arabs were quite familiar with various men claiming to be prophets, and along with that claim came the natural right to political power among the faithful. Muhammad's insistence that Allah had sent him as prophet to the Arabs meant he could claim political leadership of the entire city and tribal confederation.

Eventually, the Meccans began to actively resist Muhammad and his slowly increasing number of followers. The Banu Hashim clan under the leadership of Abu Talib continued to protect Muhammad, but his followers, who were often members of other tribes and clans, suffered abuse at the hands of their own tribesmen. Some of his followers began to recant their new faith and return to their old tribal belief system. Worried both about the loss of followers and the abuse the faithful endured, Muhammad sent many of his followers to Abyssinia, modern day Ethiopia, where they could live under the protection of Abyssinia's Christian king.

The environment Muhammad faced in Mecca was difficult. He was rejected by his kinsmen and his followers suffered abuse and exile. He

---

4 Qur'an 2:256. The verse, which says "there is no compulsion in religion," is now highly controversial. Most Islamic authorities contend the verse has been abrogated, or cancelled, by the "verse of the sword," Qur'an 9:5, which reads, "When the [four] forbidden months are over, wherever you encounter the idolaters, kill them, seize them, besiege them, wait for them at every lookout post; but if they turn [to God], maintain the prayer, and pay the prescribed alms, let them go on their way, for God is most forgiving and merciful."

desperately desired reconciliation with the Meccans and an opportunity presented itself. Some of the Meccan leaders suggested a bargain. They would bestow upon Muhammad wealth, a good marriage, and a position of importance in the tribe if he would only mention their three goddesses in his revelations. Shortly, the following was revealed to Muhammad -

> Have you thought about al-Lat and al-Uzza and Manat, the third? These are the high flying swans whose intercession is accepted with approval. (53:19-20 in its original form)

The Meccans were happy to hear Muhammad affirm the reality of their goddesses and the efficacy of prayers offered to them. Muhammad prostrated himself in prayer and the Meccans joined him. The Muslims in Abyssinia received word of this reconciliation and began their return home. But the peace did not last long. Gabriel appeared once again to Muhammad, scolding him for allowing Satan to reveal a message through him. Gabriel revealed to Muhammad the correct version of the passage, which now appears in the Qur'an as follows -

> [Disbelievers], consider al-Lat and al-Uzza, and the third one, Manat - are you to have the male and He the female? That would be a most unjust distribution! - these are nothing but names you have invented yourselves, you and your forefathers. God has sent no authority for them. These people merely follow guesswork and the whims of their souls ... (53:19-23 as it appears now)

The Meccans were furious and withdrew their offer. The verbal assaults on Muhammad increased. Muhammad was distraught and depressed at having been duped by Satan. The Muslims, who were returning to Mecca from Abyssinia, did not know whether to continue or turn back. But Allah comforted Muhammad in his travails with another revelation -

> We have never sent any messenger or prophet before you [Muhammad] into whose wishes Satan did not insinuate something, but God removes what Satan insinuates and then God affirms His message. God is all knowing and wise: ... (22:52)

This account has been called "The Satanic Verses." It appears in authoritative Islamic texts during the first four centuries of Islam. During these early centuries, no one questioned the veracity of the account and it was universally accepted. Eventually, Muslim scholars realized the implications of the "Satanic Verses" account to the legitimacy of Islam. Questions arose such as how it was that Muhammad could not distinguish between Gabriel and Satan. If he could not distinguish between them how do we know that other verses of the Qur'an, even most or all of them, did not come from Satan? Muhammad must have been able to distinguish between them if Islam is truly the religion of Allah. But then the question arises, if he could distinguish between Gabriel and Satan, such that Muhammad would instantly reject any words from Satan, what was the source of the Satanic Verses? If it was not Allah or Satan, would it not have been Muhammad himself? If so, how do we know which verses of the Qur'an are from Allah and which are from Muhammad? In short, the theological implications became clear. If Islam was to remain a legitimate religion the entire account had to be rejected. In fact, Islamic orthodoxy today completely rejects the account of the Satanic Verses. This aversion to the account is so thorough and so visceral that the Ayatollah Khomeini of Iran issued a *fatwa*, or legal judgment, authorizing the murder of British author Salman Rushdie. What did Rushdie do? He had the audacity to title one of his novels *The Satanic Verses*.

Non-Muslim scholars almost universally accept the historical accuracy of the account. They cite the widespread and uncritical rendition of the account in all the early and authoritative Islamic sources. They also cite the universal acceptance of it by Muslims for the first several centuries of Islam. Finally, they rely on the extreme unlikelihood that Muslims would have invented the account or had it foisted upon them by critics of Islam. They also cite the Qur'an *sura* 22, verse 52, comforting and reassuring Muhammad that Satan inserts something into the message of every prophet, but God is faithful to remove whatever Satan inserts. After all, from what did Muhammad need such comfort and reassurance if not from the incident of the Satanic Verses?

In any event, the persecution of Muslims continued. As long as the clan leader, Abu Talib, was around to assert his authority and insist on Muhammad's protection, Muhammad's own situation, as opposed to that of his followers, was bearable. But the persecution reached a critical point when Abu Talib died and was replaced by Abu Lahab. Abu Lahab had been an opponent of Muhammad and now as clan leader had an unrestrained hand. He removed the clan's protection from Muhammad, in essence declaring "open season" to Muhammad's opponents. Allah pronounced a particularly harsh curse upon Abu Lahab for his ill-treatment of Muhammad. The Qur'an says of him:

> May the hands of Abu Lahab be ruined! May he be ruined too! Neither his wealth nor his gains will help him: he will burn in the Flaming Fire – and so will his wife, the firewood-carrier, with a palm-fibre rope around her neck. (111)

The Hijra

Muhammad realized his life was threatened. He and his followers migrated to Medina, a city north of Mecca. This migration is known as the *hijra*. From this migration in AD 622 the fortunes of Muhammad and his small band of followers began to change and the "Islamic era" began. Medina had been torn apart by tribal conflict for decades. These conflicts had become so bad that people were afraid to go outside their homes for fear of ambush by other tribes. The Medinese realized that a neutral third-party mediator was necessary to negotiate a truce. Muhammad was the perfect candidate. Muhammad agreed to serve such a role but insisted the citizens of Medina recognize him as their leader, affirm his prophetic role, and become Muslims. Many did so. Those from the three tribes of Jews in the city were particularly absent from the group of converts.

Muhammad's Years in Medina

Muhammad transformed the fractured Medinese society into a new identity. The Muslims were no longer members of their historic tribes but were members of a new tribe. Tribal loyalties and oaths of protection now flowed to other Muslims, who formed a new communal identity. This new identity, which in Muslim conception was one of equality and the complete absence of class or status, was not quite the utopia imagined today. Those Muslims who migrated from Mecca with Muhammad were called *muhajirun* and were entitled to special privileges. Those among the Medinese who converted were called the *ansar*, or "helpers." The distinction between the groups, and the disparate treatment among them, was a source of conflict in the early Muslim community. The *ansar* had opened their homes to the *muhajirun*, supported them financially, and did not appreciate being treated as second class citizens.

The murmuring among the *ansar* concerning special privileges of the *muhajirun* was a situation that needed a resolution. The answer was not long in coming. Non-Muslims were now characterized as outsiders whose lives and property were fair game. Led by their new chief Muhammad, Muslim bands began venturing out to raid passing caravans. During the first eighteen months after the *hijra*, Muhammad led seven campaigns against Meccan caravans. The campaigns were seen as a source of wealth for the new Muslim community, a chance to repay the Meccans for their ill-treatment of the Muslims, and a chance for Muhammad to assert his new authority.

Nothing much became of these first seven campaigns. There was little fighting, no bloodshed, and no spoils taken. The only real result was to irritate the Meccans and provide a warning of what was possible in the future. But this was to change. Muhammad sent out a force with instructions to ambush a Meccan caravan at Nakhlah. This expedition, known as the Expedition of Nakhlah, resulted in one Meccan caravan attendant's death, the taking of several prisoners, and the theft of the caravan's goods.[5]

The event stirred up much controversy among the Muslims, as well as anger among the Meccans. The attack and murder of the caravan attendant occurred during the holy month of Rajab, during which raiding and killing were prohibited. Muhammad began taking criticism for his violation of this sacred tradition. However, Allah was quick to extricate Muhammad from this uncomfortable situation, revealing the following verse -

> They ask you [Prophet] about fighting in the prohibited
> month. Say, 'Fighting in that month is a great offence,
> but to bar others from God's path, to disbelieve in Him,

---

5   Later edits to the historical accounts change the import of Muhammad's instructions to the raiders from "ambush" to "keep a watch and report back" in order to remove from Muhammad the responsibility for the bloodshed and violation of the holy month.

> prevent access to the Sacred Mosque, and expel its people,
> are still greater offences in God's eyes: persecution is worse
> than killing.' (2:217)

Thus Muhammad was justified, because in the eyes of Allah, what the Meccans did in running the Muslims out of town was worse than what the Muslims did in killing them during the holy month.

The Meccans realized their caravan trade was in jeopardy, as the Muslims were now a very real threat to the northern routes. This bubbling conflict came to a head in what is known as the Battle of Badr. The Meccans had a huge caravan returning from Syria, which would need to pass through the strip of land between Medina and the Red Sea. The Meccans got word the Muslims had amassed an army of a little over 300 men intending to ambush the caravan at a well called Badr. The Meccans responded by sending out their own army of around 950 men to protect the caravan and divert it to an alternate route in hopes of eluding the ambush. The caravan did escape. This left the Meccans with a decision. Some argued the reason for their force was eliminated as the caravan had made it past Medina in safety. Others argued that this was the perfect opportunity to teach Muhammad and the Muslims a lesson. The Meccans proceeded, but when the battle turned in favor of the Muslims, the Meccans fled.

The Muslim victory was a boon for Muhammad. Lots of spoils were taken, relieving some of the economic distress in Medina. Included in the spoils were a number of Meccan soldiers, who could be ransomed for money. At least two of the prisoners were executed. A man named 'Uqbah b. Abi Mu'ayt had been particularly hostile to Muhammad back in Mecca and had written poetry critical of him. Muhammad ordered him beheaded, but right before the blade fell, 'Uqbah asked, "Who will take care of my children?" Muhammad replied, "Hell."[6]

The victory also signaled to the surrounding tribes that perhaps the Muslims had become more powerful than the Meccans. The Muslims themselves saw the victory as a vindication of Muhammad as a true prophet and Islam as Allah's favored religion. Hold-outs among the Medinese now submitted, and various tribes in the area shifted their allegiance to Muhammad.

---

6   Alfred Guillaume, *The Life of Muhammad: A Translation of Ibn Ishaq's* Sirat Rasul Allah (Oxford: Oxford University Press, 1955) page 308.

Still troubling to Muhammad were the Jewish tribes of Medina. They made fun of Muhammad and the Muslims not knowing in which direction to face while praying without having been taught by the Jews. Upon Muhammad hearing these jests, a revelation came directing him to change the direction of prayer from Jerusalem to the Kabah in Mecca.

> The foolish people will say, 'What has turned them away from the prayer direction they used to face?' Say, 'East and West belong to God. He guides whoever He will to the right way.' ... We only made the direction the one you used to face [Prophet] in order to distinguish those who follow the Messenger from those who turn on their heels: that test was hard, except for those God has guided... Turn your face in the direction of the Sacred Mosque: wherever you [believers] may be, turn your faces to it. Those who were given the Scripture know with certainty that this is the Truth from their Lord: ... (2:142-144)

This break with the Jews over the common direction of prayer was indicative of a changed attitude of Muhammad toward the Jews. The first Jewish tribe to feel his wrath was the Banu Qaynuqa, perhaps the most powerful commercial tribe in Medina. When the Muslims arrived in Medina, the Jewish tribes signed an agreement with Muhammad to support him against anyone who might attack. When the Battle of Badr was over, Muhammad challenged them to accept Islam or God would bring upon them the retribution he visited on the Meccans. Some of the Banu Qaynuqa responded that if Muhammad had faced them in battle, the outcome might have been different. At this point, Gabriel revealed to Muhammad the following verse -

> And if you learn of [fear] treachery on the part of any people, throw their treaty back at them, for God does not love the treacherous. (8:58, bracketed word reflects a common alternate translation)

Muhammad's reaction to this revelation was that he feared the Banu Qaynuqa. Based on this justification, Muhammad ordered the Muslims to lay siege to the area of the city inhabited by the Banu Qaynuqa. No one was allowed in or out for fifteen days, resulting in extreme hunger and exhaustion. The people finally came out of their houses and submitted to Muhammad. They were shackled and Muhammad ordered them all executed. One of the Arabs intervened and insisted that they had fought alongside his tribe in past battles, and should not be wasted in a single morning. Muhammad hesitated until the man grabbed him by the collar, shook him, and insisted that Muhammad let them go. Muhammad was infuriated but relented. He ordered them exiled and all of their belongings distributed between himself and the Muslims.

Muslim scholars defend the action of Muhammad by claiming the Banu Qaynuqa violated the terms of the treaty when they failed to go out with the Muslims to fight the Meccans at Badr. But most of the Muslims likewise stayed home and it is acknowledged that the Muslim force was surprised by the appearance of the Meccan army. One wonders how the Banu Qaynuqa could have known the Meccans would be there, invoking their duty to fight for Muhammad, if Muhammad and the Muslims didn't know it either.

The Muslims continued busying themselves with raids on tribes in the area, on Meccan caravans, and in dealing with the direct danger they faced with a now vigilant Mecca. Certain tribes began arriving in Medina to pledge submission to Muhammad. The Meccans defeated the Muslims in the next battle they fought, the Battle of Uhud, and Muhammad was seriously wounded. This created uncertainty in Muhammad's increasingly powerful position.

Muhammad did not feel completely secure in Medina as long as two Jewish tribes remained who refused to convert and pledge obedience to him. Muhammad first addressed his attention to the Banu al-Nadir. They were the wealthiest of the remaining Jews, owning significant lands containing date palms. Muhammad ordered siege be laid against the Banu al-Nadir until they surrendered and he sent them into exile with only what they could carry. Their remaining possessions were divided among the Muslims. The Banu al-Nadir migrated to Khaybar, a city in the region with a significant Jewish population.

The Meccans launched what they hoped would be one final assault on the Muslims in Medina. The Meccans amassed a large force of soldiers from Mecca itself and from among the still-allied tribes. The Muslims were terrified at the size of the Meccan army but help was readily present. A

Persian in their midst who had been a slave, but freed upon his conversion to Islam, advised Muhammad of a battle tactic used successfully by the Persian Empire. The Muslims followed his advice and built a trench across the boundary of the city that was vulnerable to attack. When the Meccans arrived, neither the men nor their horses and camels had seen such a thing before. The trench completely stalled them. Uncertain what to do, and after a delay of several days with only minor volleying and shouting of insults, the Meccan army melted away. This event is known as the Battle of the Trench.

At last Muhammad was in a position to deal with the final Jewish tribe of Medina, the Banu Qurayzah. The Islamic sources say that prior to the Battle of the Trench, upon seeing the approaching Meccan army, the Banu Qurayzah decided to hedge their bets. They negotiated with the Meccans about their fate should the Meccans defeat the Muslims. The Banu Qurayzah did not assist the Meccans in any way, and actually aided the Muslims by helping dig the trench, but their lack of complete commitment to the Islamic cause was more than Muhammad could take. Upon learning of their negotiations with the Meccans, Muhammad attacked the Banu Qurayzah, who escaped to their homes. The Muslims laid siege on them for a month. Finally exhausted, they pleaded for mercy, asking that Muhammad send them into exile as he had done the prior tribes. Muhammad demanded they surrender unconditionally. They did so. Muhammad ordered that trenches be dug in the middle of the city and ordered that every man and every boy who had reached puberty be beheaded. Historians estimate the number of beheaded at between 600 and 900. The women and children were taken as slaves, with Muhammad having the first choice among the women. The tribe's possessions were divided among the Muslims.

The Muslims were now completely united and had obtained through raids or voluntary submission the allegiance of many of the area tribes. They proceeded to Mecca to make the annual pilgrimage. They were stopped at the gates by the Meccans and negotiations resulted in the Treaty of Hudaiba. The treaty provided, among other things, that there would be peace between the Meccans and Muslims for ten years, and that the Meccans would vacate the city each succeeding year to allow the Muslims to make the pilgrimage unmolested. The Muslims were furious at Muhammad having allowed to pass an excellent opportunity to attack and defeat the Meccans. A revelation came down addressing the situation -

> Truly We have opened up a path to clear triumph for you
> [Prophet] … God was pleased with the believers … and
> rewarded them with a speedy triumph and many future
> gains. God is mighty and wise. He has promised you
> [people] many future gains: He has hastened this gain for
> you. He has held back the hands of hostile people from you
> as a sign for the faithful and He will guide you to a straight
> path. There are many other gains [to come], over which
> you have no power. God has full control over them: God
> has power over all things. (48:1, 18-19, 20-21)

The promised gain was not long in coming. Muhammad led the Muslims on a raid of the largely Jewish city of Khaybar. Muslim scholars note that Muhammad believed the Jews of Khaybar were conspiring against the Muslims, which justified the following events. The Muslim troops began attacking fortresses in a piecemeal fashion, taking captives and spoils along the way. As the Muslim forces neared the final fortresses in the city they brought to Muhammad a man named Kinanah. Kinanah was the custodian of the treasure of the city. Muhammad demanded he reveal the location of the treasure. Kinanah refused. Muhammad ordered "torture him until you root out what he has."[7] The soldiers kindled a fire on Kinanah's chest until he almost died, and then he was beheaded.

That night a woman of Khaybar, who had been widowed that day, offered to cook dinner for Muhammad. Muhammad accepted the offer but discovered after taking a bite that the meat had been poisoned. He spit out the bite saying, "This bone informs me that it has been poisoned."[8] Islamic orthodoxy says, however, that Muhammad died from this poisoning close to five years later.

The Muslims continued to increase in strength as more tribes acquiesced in the face of attacks or voluntarily submitted to Muhammad. In the process they became Muslims. In the eighth year after the *hijra*, the Muslims gathered a massive army and marched to Mecca. The Meccans saw the inevitable outcome and surrendered. No one was killed except those who were particularly harsh in their earlier criticism of Muhammad.

---

7   *The History of al-Tabari*, volume VIII, "The Victory of Islam," translated by Michael Fishbein (Albany, State University of New York Press, 1997), page 123.

8   Id., page 124.

Muhammad was now not only prophet of Arabia but political ruler of most of it. His final sermon in Mecca is worth reproducing in full.

> O people, listen to my words. I do not know whether I shall ever meet you again in this place after this year. O people, your blood and your property are sacrosanct until you meet your Lord, just as this day and this month of yours are sacred. Surely you will meet your Lord and He will question you about your deeds. I have [already] made this known. "Let he who has a pledge return it to the one who entrusted him with it;' (2:283; 4:58) all usury is abolished, but 'your capital' belongs to you. Wrong not and you shall not be wronged.' God has decreed that there will be no usury, and the usury of Abbas b. 'Abd al-Muttalib is abolished, all of it. All bloodshed in the pre-Islamic days is to be left unavenged…Time has completed its cycle [and is] as it was on the day that God created the heavens and the earth. 'The number of the months with God is twelve: [they were] in the Book of God on the day He created the heavens and the earth. Four of them are sacred, (9:36) the three consecutive [months] and the Rajab, [which is called the month of] Mudar, which is between Jumada [II] and Sha'ban."
>
> "Now then, O people, you have a right over your wives and they have a right over you. You have [the right] that they should not cause any one of whom you dislike to tread your beds; and that they should not commit any open indecency. If they do, then God permits you to shut them in separate rooms and to beat them, but not severely. If they abstain from [evil], they have the right to their food and clothing in accordance with custom. **Treat women well, for they are [like] domestic animals ('awan) with you and do not possess anything for themselves.** You have taken them only as a trust from God, and you have made the enjoyment of their persons lawful by the word of God, so understand and listen to my words, O people. I have conveyed the Message, and have left you with something which, if you hold fast to it, you will never go astray: that

is, the Book of God and the sunnah of the Prophet. Listen to my words, O people, for I have conveyed the Message and understand [it]. Know for certain that every Muslim is a brother of another Muslim, and that all Muslims are brethren. It is not lawful for a person [to take] from his brother except that which he has given him willingly, so do not wrong yourselves. O God, have I not conveyed the message?' It was reported [to me] that the people said, 'O God, yes' and the Messenger of God said, 'O God, bear witness.'"[9]

Succession to Muhammad

While on his death bed, Muhammad asked that he be brought writing materials so he could write something which, if followed, would never lead the people astray. For reasons not identified in the Muslim literature, the people wrangled and delayed over this request. Muhammad died before he could write anything. Most theorize he intended to name his successor. Before he died, his last command to those around his bed was to drive out all polytheists from the Arabian Peninsula.

Two groups vied for the right to name the successor to Muhammad. One group believed the successor would not only become the new political leader of the Islamic community but also the spiritual successor. They saw a special spiritual blessing or character in Muhammad himself so that only a descendant could claim rule. This group proposed Ali, from Muhammad's household, as the natural candidate. Others, most notably those recent converts to Islam from Mecca, desired to regain their positions of prominence in the new community. They desired only a political leader, one from among their own. They proposed Abu Bakr, the elderly and very close friend of Muhammad.

The decision was based on political maneuvering rather than on any sort of well-deliberated consensus. This created a rift within the Islamic

---

9   *The History of al-Tabari*, volume IX, "The Last Years of the Prophet," translated by Ismail K. Poonawala (Albany: State University of New York Press, 1990), page 88 (bold text by the author). The reader will note the reference to treating women as domestic animals has been edited from later renditions of the sermon, probably to rehabilitate Muhammad's attitude toward women and remove the source of offense.

community that exists until today. Those who supported Ali became known as the Shi'ites. Those that supported Abu Bakr are known as Sunnis. These groups fought and feuded throughout the early period of Islam and still to this day do not regard the other as true Muslims.

Sunnis and Shi'ites

Sunnis are by far the majority of Muslims in the world and predominate everywhere but Iran. Shi'ites are the majority in Iran and Iraq. Shi'ites believe in the perpetual succession of Muhammad in the form of a human on earth who is filled with a special spiritual blessing from Allah, and is thus the righteous and worthy guide for all of mankind. Ali became the fourth caliph, or successor, following Abu Bakr, Omar, and Uthman. Shi'ites believe he was the first true successor to Muhammad. They identify eleven other caliphs after Ali. They say this twelfth caliph, also called the twelfth imam, never died but became hidden in the spiritual realms. He exists in the spiritual world to communicate with and guide the temporal leader of the faithful. The most well-known of these temporal imams was Ayatollah Khomeini, who led the revolution in Iran to overthrow the Shah, and later became the supreme ruler himself. He was succeeded by Ayatollah Khamenei, the current supreme leader in Iran.

According to the Shi'ites, humanity will always have divine guidance through the temporal imam who operates similarly to the Catholic Pope. Due to communication with the invisible twelfth imam the temporal leader is infallible in his pronouncements on Islamic belief and practice. This also means he holds extraordinary political power as well, which is not surprising given his role as political, as well as spiritual, successor to Muhammad.

Sunnis see all of this as heretical. They view the caliphate as only political succession to Muhammad so that Shi'ite imams have no special status whatsoever. They do not regard any intermediaries between Allah and his creation, and clergy fill no role other than guides and teachers. Sunnis of the Wahabi variety, such as those in Saudi Arabia, see the Shi'ite beliefs as sacrilege, as diverting to men some of the honor and authority that belong to Allah alone. They believe such constitutes polytheism, the gravest sin of Islam, and an offense that takes one outside the community of faith.

Conflict and violence in the Middle East have many causes. But looking beneath the surface one can usually identify animosity between Sunnis and Shi'ites as a factor.

The Wars of Apostasy

After the death of Muhammad many of the tribes that had associated themselves with the Muslims fell away. Some rejected Islam altogether, apparently believing their oaths of loyalty were personal to Muhammad, and not to Islam as a religion. Some tribes maintained their Islamic religion, to whatever extent they understood it, but refused to continue paying taxes to Medina in accordance with their prior oaths of loyalty. Other tribes, Christian, Jew and pagan, had never submitted to Muhammad and the Muslims. These tribes became targets of aggression in accordance with Muhammad's deathbed command to rid the peninsula of all polytheists.

Under the leadership of the first caliph, Abu Bakr, the Muslim armies set out to reconvert those tribes that had fallen away, force those that had stopped paying taxes to begin doing so again, and to destroy any tribe that was not Muslim.[10] Rather than lose one's life in these battles, one could convert or reconvert to Islam, and pay the taxes to Medina that the Muslims required. Some of the threats used to subdue the tribes and reconvert them were less than noble. In one instance, the emissary sent by Abu Bakr to warn a tribe of the consequences of their failure to convert, told the tribe, "There is coming to you a man who will violate your womenfolk. Indeed, you will nickname him 'the Greatest Stud.' So it is your business."[11] Over the next couple of years, the entire Arabian Peninsula was subdued for Islam through these often brutal and bloody military campaigns.

---

10   These wars are known as the "Wars of Apostasy" or by their Arabic name, the *Ridda* wars. In addition to Muhammad's deathbed command to rid the peninsula of all but Muslims, the wars are also justified by Muhammad's command to kill anyone who leaves Islam. See *Sahih Bukhari* 83:17 and *Sahih Muslim* 16:4152.

11   *The History of al-Tabari*, volume X, "The Conquest of the Arabs," translated by Fred McGraw Donner (Albany: State University of New York Press, 1993), page 61.

The Expansion of Islam

Once the Arabian Peninsula was conquered, the Muslim armies turned their sights on Arab tribes loyal to either the Christian Byzantine Empire to the northwest or to the Zoroastrian Persian Empire to the northeast. These tribes served as buffers between the wild and warlike nomadic tribes in the Arabian Peninsula and the settled towns and villages of these two great empires.

The Byzantine and Persian armies had fought each other for many decades, moving the boundary between their empires back and forth as the armies took turns with the upper hand. By all accounts, both armies were exhausted and had lost the will to continue fighting. Further, during the sixth and early seventh centuries, bubonic plague ravaged the cities and towns of the region, killing thirty percent or more of the population. The plague was carried by fleas living on rats. The desert regions were immune since there were no hiding places for the rats or forage on which they could feed. Finally, a great theological divide had stricken the Byzantine Empire over the nature of the person of Christ. Did he have two natures, both divine and human in one person, as the ecclesiastic authorities and Greek-speaking cities believed, or did he have only one, divine nature, as the towns, villages and countryside believed? The central authorities forced their view on the towns and countryside with an oppressive hand.

These historical factors made the Byzantine and Persian armies easy work for the Muslim forces after they had finished off the Arab tribes of the border. After defeating an army, one purpose of which was to protect a region of settled towns and villages, the Muslims established garrisons from which they ruled the surrounding countryside. With some glaring and horrifying exceptions, the general populace was unharmed. In some instances, the Muslim armies were seen as liberators from the oppressive ecclesiastical authorities. The common people were not forcibly converted to Islam. Rather, the non-Muslim population was forced to pay the *jizya*, a tax designed to humiliate and subdue them. The non-Muslims were also treated as clearly second-class citizens. Over time, the non-Muslims converted to Islam. They desired to avoid the heavy tax burden and the discrimination they suffered. They also desired to gain a share of the spoils of war from distant conquests which were divided among Muslims.

These wars allowed Islam to spread very rapidly through the Middle East, North Africa and Central Asia, establishing what we now recognize as the heart of the Muslim world. Muslim forces crossed at Gibraltar into Spain and their northward march was eventually stopped in Tours, France by the forces of Charles Martel in October 732. The Muslims were content to occupy Spain for nearly 800 years. The eastward march was stopped not so much by military defeat as by internal political conflicts.

CHAPTER 2
The Five Pillars of Islam

MUSLIMS VIEW FIVE PRACTICES to constitute the "pillars" of their faith. Any Muslim who does not recognize these 'pillars' as fundamental requirements of the Islamic faith is not considered a true Muslim. The five pillars are the confession of faith, ritual prayer, fasting, giving alms, and the pilgrimage.

The Confession of Faith

The Islamic confession of faith, or *shahada*, is the first pillar of Islam. Recited in Arabic, the confession is simple: "There is no god but God, and Muhammad is the messenger of God." Practicing Muslim parents whisper this phrase into the ears of newborns. Muslims whisper this phrase under their breath at times of stress or trial. And converts to Islam are to pronounce this, with actual belief and intention, to formalize their conversion.

Ritual Prayer

The Islamic ritual prayer, or *salat*, is performed five times per day. Probably more than anything else, ritual prayer identifies one as a Muslim.

It is mandatory for every Muslim. To deny its compulsory nature is to deny the faith and make one an apostate.

According to legend, while Muhammad still lived in Mecca, he had a vision in the night. In the vision, Gabriel accompanied him as he rode a winged mule to the "farthest mosque," or the temple in Jerusalem, where he offered prayers and was offered wine and milk. He chose the milk as wine is prohibited in Islam. From there he traveled up through the seven heavens meeting various prophets along the way, until finally reaching God in the highest heaven. Here God commanded Muhammad to instruct the Muslims to perform the ritual prayer fifty times per day. On his way back down through the various levels of heaven, Moses asked him how many times he was commanded to pray. On hearing the number, Moses sent him back up to request a reduction in the number. God reduced the number, but Moses was still not pleased. So the process was repeated over and over until God had lowered the number to five times per day. Moses asked Muhammad to go back up one more time, but Muhammad refused, saying five was an acceptable number.

Most Muslims claim this was a literal, physical journey, as the Qur'an says:

> Glory to Him who made His servant travel by night from
> the sacred place of worship to the furthest place of worship,
> whose surroundings We have blessed, to show him some
> of Our signs . . (17:1)

Muslim scholars identify the "farthest place of worship" as the temple in Jerusalem, and in multiple sources Muhammad describes the building in great detail. However the temple had been destroyed in AD 70, centuries before this alleged journey. Others claim the building was the al-Aqsa mosque, but this was not constructed until AD 691, many decades after the alleged journey.

In performing the five daily prayers, Muslims must face the direction of the Kabah in Mecca. Muslims must make a sincere effort to accurately locate the direction of the Kabah from their current location. If one is uncertain about the direction and makes no effort to find it, his prayer is invalid, even if by chance he prays in the right direction.

Mosques are built so the directional prayer marker, the *qibla*, is in the front of the prayer hall. Thus, as worshippers arrange themselves in lines facing the front, they are properly aligned toward Mecca. The direction toward Mecca is itself sacred, as Muhammad commanded Muslims not to face or turn their backs to the Kabah when answering the call of nature.

Before offering the prayer, the Muslim must obtain a sacred state of purity, which results from ritual washing. This washing is called *wudu*. Islamic law provides strict rules concerning the manner of such washing, including rules on the nature of the water used to wash. While there are differences in details among the various schools of Islamic law, generally speaking, one washes the hands to the elbows, washes the face, rubs wet hands over the head, and washes the feet to the ankle, right before left. Mosques contain special rooms wherein one performs this ritual washing. On occasion, a mosque will have a fountain outside in a courtyard where Muslims will wash.

Islam also allows for "washing" with dirt if water is not available. As one might expect, there are rules concerning what types of dirt are appropriate for such washing.

After washing, the Muslim must be careful not to engage in certain activities which will invalidate the washing and require its repetition. The various schools of Islamic law have slightly different rules on this issue, but generally speaking, the following are of concern: touching a dog, a pig, blood, a corpse, semen or pus, answering the call of nature, passing wind, losing consciousness, touching a woman, touching one's own private parts, vomiting and laughter.

The times of the five daily prayers are also regulated. They occur just before dawn, in the early afternoon, late afternoon, just after sunset, and at night. Strict rules govern the beginning and ending times of each prayer based on the position of the sun in the sky. These times are announced by the *muezzin*, who calls from the top of the spire at the mosque, called the minaret. In most of the Muslim world today, the call to prayer is recorded and broadcast by loudspeaker.

The prayer must be performed at a pure location. Inside the mosque is pure. The bottom of one's shoe is defiled, so worshippers remove their shoes before entering the mosque. But what about prayer offered outside the mosque? The ground is considered impure, so Muslims must place something between them and the ground or floor. Usually small carpets do the trick, but in the absence of a carpet, even newspaper will do.

The prayer begins with the worshipper standing alert and reciting *Allah akbar* ("God is great") and then the *Fatiha*, the first *sura* of the

Qur'an. Subsequent movements include bending over and placing one's hands on the knees, kneeling, and then prostrating with the toes, knees, elbows, hands, and forehead on the ground. Returning to the standing position constitutes one *rakat*, or repetition. Each of the five daily prayers involves a different number of repetitions, two in the early morning, three at sundown, and four in the others.

Muhammad also ordered Muslims not to look toward the sky during prayer. According to *Sahih Bukhari* 12:717, "Narrated Anas bin Malik: The Prophet said, 'What is wrong with those people who look towards the sky during the prayer?' His talk grew stern while delivering this speech and he said, 'They should stop (looking towards the sky during the prayer); otherwise their eye-sight would be taken away.'"

Women must be segregated from the men. In the mosque, this usually means a separate entrance and a prayer area screened off from the men, yet still allowing the women to hear the voice of the mullah when he preaches. The reason for the segregation is both spiritual and practical. Practically, the mixture of men and women in the position of prostration might easily lead to distraction and impure thoughts. The spiritual reason is that a woman, donkey or dog passing between the worshipper and the *qibla* invalidates a man's prayer.[12]

Prayers are invalidated by the same things that invalidate the washing. But, there are additional things that will invalidate the prayer. One must not speak, clear one's throat (except to correct the prayer leader for any mistake in reciting the Qur'an), return the greeting of *salaam*, eat or drink, or engage in any action that would indicate to an onlooker that one is not praying. A man must not wear gold jewelry or silk clothing during prayer or the prayer will be invalid. Any clothing worn must not be contaminated with impurities such as bodily fluids. A woman is considered unclean during her menstrual cycle. Her prayers during this time are void.

Congregational prayer in the mosque during the early afternoon prayer time on Fridays is either compulsory or emphatically recommended for all Muslims, depending on the school of law one follows. It is not required for women. The prayer leader must be a man. Attendance at the Friday prayer earns a Muslim more spiritual merit than any other prayer during the week. Praying the ritual prayer serves to forgive sins. Among the most

12   See *Sahih Bukhari* 9:490 and *Sahih Muslim* 4:1034

conservative Muslims, all shops, offices and stores must be closed during the Friday prayer. Failure to do so in Saudi Arabia is a criminal offense.

Ritual Fasting

Muslims are required to fast from sunrise to sunset every day during the month of Ramadan. Strictly speaking, the time of fasting begins when one can distinguish a dark thread from a light one in the palm of one's hand, and ends when one can no longer distinguish between the threads. This rule was borrowed from Judaism. Since the Islamic calendar is lunar, the time of year in which Ramadan falls each year changes relative to the solar calendar, moving forward a few days each year. Thus, Ramadan sometimes falls during the middle of summer, when days are the longest, making the fasting period very difficult. Sometimes it falls in the middle of winter when the days are short.

During the fasting period each day, Muslims are not to eat, drink, smoke, have sexual relations, receive an injection, or in the opinion of one school of law, inhale in the midst of a dense cloud of suspended dust. Muslim scholars debate whether swallowing one's own saliva, taking required medication, drinking water to swallow prescription pills, and other such acts, violate the fast. Violation of the fast requires one to make up that day's fast at a later time, and may also require one to make atonement for the violation through feeding a needy person.

There are exceptions to the requirement of fasting. The fast of a menstruating woman is invalid, as is the fast of a woman who bleeds after giving birth. One who is traveling need not fast, provided the trip begins before dawn and covers at least forty miles. Those who are ill or very elderly need not fast, but must feed a needy person for every day of fasting missed.

Ramadan is a very festive month for Muslims. When the fast is over each day, Muslims visit family and friends, wear new clothes and give each other gifts. Each night they will enjoy a feast, and the merry-making usually lasts well into the early morning hours. There is a tremendous sense of communal solidarity during Ramadan due to shared sacrifice and shared celebration. Non-Muslims living in Muslim lands are not required to fast, but often will want to join in the experiences of their Muslim friends. Restaurants and cafes close during the daylight hours of Ramadan, and in some cases, it is a criminal offense to eat or drink within the eyesight of a fasting Muslim.

Muslims also observe voluntary fasts, which are recommended on the thirteenth through the fifteenth of the month, Mondays, and Thursdays. Fridays and Saturdays are disapproved for fasting.

Alms

Muslims are required to give 2.5 percent of their excess wealth to charity. "Excess" wealth is defined as that income remaining after one has paid all of one's bills and accounted for all other living expenses.

The Pilgrimage

The final pillar of Islam is the pilgrimage to Mecca, known as the *hajj*. Every adult Muslim who is able must make the pilgrimage once in their lives. The pilgrimage involves travelling to Mecca in a sacred condition and performing a series of rituals over the course of several days. (Non-Muslims are not allowed in Mecca so as to prevent their defiling the holy places of Islam.) The sacred state includes having performed special washings and men wearing a seamless white cotton wrap and sandals. If no sandals are available, he may wear shoes with the backs cut out. The rituals include walking around the Kabah seven times counterclockwise and "greeting" a black stone set into the outer wall of the Kabah. Then pilgrims move swiftly between the hills of Safa and Marwah to commemorate Hagar's frantic search for water for Ishmael. They then throw pebbles at three stone pillars, representing the rejection of Satan, and sacrifice an animal. Today's pilgrimage involves so many people that the animal sacrifices are done by proxy by local butchers.

If a Muslim is unable to make the pilgrimage due to physical disability, he or she may pay a proxy to make the pilgrimage on his or her behalf. There is disagreement over what is meant by the requirement that the Muslim be "able" to make the pilgrimage. It is generally agreed that "ability" encompasses physical, mental and financial ability. There is also disagreement on the requirement for a woman who has no male to accompany her.

CHAPTER 3
Authorities

THE QUR'AN IS THE ultimate source of authority in every Muslim's life. Following closely thereafter is the example of Muhammad. His words and deeds are recorded in the *hadith*. Islamic law, or *shari'a*, governs all aspects of a Muslim's individual life and the life of the Muslim community. *Shari'a* is derived from the Qur'an and the *hadith*.

The Qur'an

The Qur'an is the holy book of Islam, and the collection of the revelations Muhammad received from Gabriel. The Qur'an is divided into *suras*, or chapters, and verses, and is about eighty percent the size of the New Testament. The Qur'an only exists in Arabic, the language of its revelation. Translations are not considered "the Qur'an" but only a type of commentary on the Qur'an. Muslims believe the Qur'an is a word-for-word copy of an eternal, uncreated book in heaven which contains a verbatim record of God's speech. Thus, the Qur'an itself is a verbatim record of God's actual speech and is absolutely perfect and without any error. It is the most beautiful, wise, instructive and beneficial speech known to humanity, and God's instruction book for all human belief, thought, and activity. To the Muslim, it is God's absolute truth.

Reading the Qur'an, however, is not easy. The revelations Muhammad received from Gabriel were delivered piecemeal, a few verses at a time, over a period of approximately twenty-three years. The verses were gathered in random order and placed, seemingly haphazardly, into the Qur'an. Muslims believe the angel Gabriel instructed Muhammad in what order to arrange the verses and *suras* of the Qur'an. He also met with Muhammad annually to review the previously revealed words to make sure no error had crept into either Muhammad's repetition of them, or the people's recollection and recording of them. The 114 *suras* are arranged from longest to shortest rather than chronologically or topically. In essence, reading the Qur'an is like reading the biblical book of Proverbs, where each verse is self-contained, and has no apparent relationship to the verses coming before or after.

Scholars do have a clear idea of whether a *sura* contains verses primarily revealed in Mecca or in Medina, and can order the *suras* chronologically. They do this by examining the nature of the revelations. Meccan revelations affirm the unity of God, encourage moral and ethical behavior, accommodate the beliefs and practices of Christians and Jews, encourage them to faithfully follow their own scriptures, tell stories of biblical prophets in slightly modified form, and generally try to attract believers.[13] The Medinan revelations, received once Muhammad had obtained political power, are more legislative and militaristic. They no longer affirm "People of the Book," that is, Christians and Jews, but attest that God will accept no religion but Islam.

There are a variety of accounts of how and when the various revelations were gathered together into one book. In order to minimize the possibility of mistakes having crept into the text of the Qur'an, Muslims tend to favor the earliest possible collection. However, the various accounts are impossible to harmonize and there are serious problems with the earliest reports of the Qur'an's compilation.

The favored account is that Muhammad saw to the compilation of the Qur'an during his own lifetime. This report says Muhammad gathered

---

13 The ways in which the Qur'an's version of biblical stories varies from the biblical accounts can be traced to sources such as rabbinic writings and Christian children's books pre-dating Islam. Non-Muslims scholars suggest Muhammad heard these stories recited by Christians and Jews who were repeating oral traditions of sacred stories, and who did not, or were not able to, distinguish between the biblical accounts and the human embellishments to those accounts.

together in one place the written materials on which the revelations were recorded and kept these sheets in his home. The next rendition says that some of the revelations were written by secretaries and other Muslims on palm leaves, bones, parchment, or whatever other materials were available, but most were simply memorized by the Muslims. During one of the battles of the *Ridda* wars, many of the Muslims who had memorized parts of the Qur'an were killed. This prompted Abu Bakr, the first caliph, to order a collection of the verses. He appointed Zaid ibn Thabit, one of Muhammad's secretaries, to accomplish the job. Zaid answered that if Abu Bakr had commanded him to move a mountain, it would be an easier task. Nevertheless, he undertook the job. He collected the various written material and memories of the Muslims and created a book. (If the first account were true, Zaid could have simply gone to the home of Muhammad and picked up the book Muhammad had created before he died.) Zaid's book was kept in the home of Abu Bakr, and then passed to Umar, Muhammad's second successor, and then to Umar's daughter, Hafsa. One wonders how important Muslims considered the Qur'an at this early date since it was treated so casually, and was ultimately kept among the personal belongings of the caliph's daughter.

Soon, however, there is overwhelming historical evidence that other Qur'ans that varied from Hafsa's Qur'an were circulating among different areas of the Muslim realm. A general in one of the Muslim armies noticed his soldiers, who hailed from several different areas, fighting over the correct language of the Qur'an. The general wrote Uthman, the third caliph, warning of these conflicts over the Qur'anic language and suggesting he do something about it. Uthman ordered Zaid to travel back to Medina, obtain Hafsa's copy, and with the aid of three noble assistants, determine the correct language of the Qur'an. In the event of a conflict in language between versions, he was to prefer the version used around Medina. Zaid brought his finished product to Uthman. Uthman announced that this was forevermore the "official" version and ordered all others burned. There was great anger among those who favored other versions and saw burning them as sacrilege. Eventually, Uthman's order was carried out, but not completely. Copies of the Qur'an which predate Uthman's orders have been found, compared with the official version, and significant differences noted.

It is heresy for Muslims to consider the Qur'an might contain any imperfection, or that it was not preserved exactly as Muhammad delivered it. In fact, the Qur'an itself repeatedly testifies to its own sublime perfection and inerrancy. An Iranian scholar, Ali Dashti, wrote, "… there ought to be no trace of human intellectual imperfection in anything God says."[14] Even to allow oneself to think the Qur'an might contain any mistake or material from Muhammad or any other human constitutes a very grave sin. Yet objective non-Muslim scholars find multiple historical, geographical, and scientific mistakes in the Qur'an. In addition they have found errors in Arabic grammar, apparently made to maintain a rhyming scheme, and words from foreign languages. There are completely unintelligible verses, stories in the Qur'an that trace back to human authors and instructions and teachings, commensurate with seventh-century culture, which are unfathomable in the modern world.

Muhammad

The Qur'an says of Muhammad that he is "only a warner" (22:49). Muhammad himself was not certain about his eternal destiny (46:7-9). Muhammad performed no miracles. His critics ridiculed him for failing to do so since miracles were the proof of prophethood (13:7 among many other verses). Yet over time, Muslim ideas about Muhammad grew more fantastic, and he took on superhuman status.

The Qur'an gives very little instruction to Muslims on how they should live. To be sure, the Qur'an encourages Muslims (and by extension, all humanity) to imitate Muhammad as best they can, stating among other things:

> Whoever obeys the Messenger obeys God. (4:80)
> … so accept whatever the Messenger gives you, and abstain from whatever he forbids you. (59:7)
> The Messenger of God is an excellent model for those of you who put your hope in God and the Last Day and remember Him often. (33:21)
> When God and His Messenger have decided on a matter that concerns them, it is not fitting for any believing man or woman to claim freedom of choice in that matter: whoever disobeys God and His Messenger is far astray. (33:36)

---

14   Ali Dashti, *Twenty-Three Years*, translated by F. R. C. Bagley (Costa Mesa, CA: Mazda Publishers, 1994), page 155.

Because of these instructions, Islamic theology developed the idea that Muhammad's words and actions were divinely inspired. Muslims came to see him not only as the last and greatest prophet but as perfect. Muslims believe Muhammad never acted in his own interest but always with the most noble, righteous, and selfless motives. Muhammad's life became the objective standard by which all human behavior is to be judged. Further, Muslims came to believe that Muhammad had performed, by God's permission and power, a wide variety of miracles.

Bolstering this belief that Muhammad was the centerpiece of history was the recognition that Qur'anic revelation often came at the precise moment to serve Muhammad's needs. Muhammad's favorite wife, Aisha, is widely quoted as saying, "I see that your Lord hastens to satisfy your desires."[15] We have already seen a revelation to quiet anger among Muslims when Muhammad ordered his soldiers to kill during the holy month. We also saw a revelation promising the spoils of Khaybar when Muslims complained that Muhammad should have ordered an attack of Mecca rather than signing the Treaty of Hudaiba.

Aisha's comment quoted above came after the following events. Muhammad had a rotation schedule for sleeping with each of his wives. (Because of his super sexual prowess, God allowed Muhammad alone among all human men to marry more than four wives at a time.) One night, he slept with a wife out of turn. The wife whose turn it was discovered him, causing great indignation among his wives and an embarrassing situation for Muhammad. His wives took revenge by refusing to sleep with him. After this situation became intolerable, God rescued Muhammad with the following revelation:

> You may make any of [your women] wait and receive any of them as you wish, but you will not be at fault if you invite one whose turn you have previously set aside: this way it is more likely that they will be satisfied and will not be distressed and will all be content with what you have given them. (33:51)

On another occasion, Muhammad desired Zaynab, the wife of his adopted son, after accidentally seeing her in a state of undress. His adopted

15 *Sahih Bukhari* 60:311

son offered on several occasions to divorce Zaynab so Muhammad could marry her. Initially, Muhammad refused, but finally the divorce happened and Muhammad married her.

The reaction to this apparent scheme subjected Muhammad to humiliation and scorn. But this was not to last long, as God again came to Muhammad's rescue. His marriage to Zaynab was God's divine will:

> When you [Prophet] said to the man who had been favoured by God and by you, 'Keep your wife and be mindful of God,' you hid in your heart what God would later reveal: you were afraid of people, but it is more fitting that you fear God. When Zayd no longer wanted her, We gave her to you in marriage so that there might be no fault in believers marrying the wives of their adopted sons after they no longer wanted them. God's command must be carried out: the Prophet is not at fault for what God has ordained for him. (33:37-38)

In order to further rehabilitate Muhammad's reputation after his marriage to the wife of his adopted son, Islam forbids adoption.

Apparently, God was concerned with more than protecting Muhammad's sexual desires. The Qur'an also provides:

> Believers, do not enter the Prophet's apartments for a meal unless you are given permission to do so; do not linger until [a meal] is ready. When you are invited, go in; then, when you have taken your meal, leave. Do not stay on and talk, for that would offend the Prophet. (33:53)

The inclusion of these words of approval, protection, and provision for Muhammad in the eternal, uncreated word of God could only mean one thing. It means Muhammad was the greatest, most honored, and highest of all God's creation, and no criticism or disapproval of him, or anything he did or said, would ever be tolerated. He is to be obeyed, imitated, honored, revered and venerated. Muslims think and speak of Muhammad in the highest possible terms, and only stop short of worshipping him. Such would violate the Qur'an's commands against associating partners with God.

The Hadith

Given the elevated position of Muhammad within Islam, it is no surprise that Muslims eventually realized they should create a record of his words and deeds. No one bothered while Muhammad was alive, or even in the earliest several decades of Islam. But oral traditions about his words and deeds, known as the *hadith*, began circulating by the end of the first Islamic century. As conceptions of Islamic law developed, and Muhammad's example came to be seen as an important source for that law, scholars increasingly saw the recording of those oral traditions as critical.

However, these scholars encountered a perplexing problem. The first few centuries of Islam saw debate and conflict, often violent, over differing ideas of theology and politics. A wide variety of sects vied for prominence, and political intrigue, assassinations, and quests for power were commonplace. In such an environment, as people sought to strengthen whatever claim they advocated, a disturbing practice developed. That practice was fabricating oral traditions about what Muhammad said or did and using these fabricated claims to support their position. Even pious Muslims fabricated *hadiths*. They did so whenever it aided them in illustrating a point of faith or doctrine, or when encouraging moral and ethical behavior. How were these scholars to sift the hundreds of thousands of *hadiths* and determine which were authentic and which were fabricated?

The science of *hadith* criticism was born. This process involved two prongs. The first prong was to examine the *isnad,* or chain of oral transmission. The scholar would trace the chain of transmitters, making sure each person in the chain was not a member of a sectarian movement but adhered to orthodoxy. Each person needed a reputation for honesty and piety. Each person in the chain must have known or been in the presence of both the person from whom he received the *hadith* and the person to whom he transmitted it. Scholars also looked at how widely circulated was the *hadith.* Those with a larger number of transmitters were preferred to those with only one or a few independent chains. These *hadith* scholars developed a system of grading the reliability of the *hadiths* and characterizing them in various ways according to the trustworthiness of the chain.

The second prong dealt with the content of the *hadith.* The theological presupposition was that Muhammad could never have said or done anything that was incorrect, dishonorable, or questionable. Thus, even if the *isnad* was of impeccable reliability, a *hadith* would be rejected if it put

Muhammad in a bad light. For instance, a *hadith* containing a prophecy determined to be false would be rejected as forged no matter how strong the *isnad* was. Further, to avoid the appearance of protecting Muhammad rather than engaging in a purely dispassionate search for truth, *hadith* scholars who rejected a *hadith* based on content would go back and read into the *isnad* some defect or problem. This in turn would justify rejection of the *hadith* on grounds of a faulty *isnad*.

Scholars began publishing collections of *hadiths* they evaluated as completely reliable, or *sahih*. Other categories of *hadith* are *hasan*, which means "good and trustworthy," *daif*, which means "weak," and *mawdu*, which means "forged". Generally, only *sahih* are grounds for doctrine or theology. *Hasan* and *daif* are acceptable for establishing legal rules. Of the approximately 770,000 *hadiths* in existence, the *hadith* scholar Bukhari whittled down the number to only a few thousand *sahih hadith*. In addition to *Sahih Bukhari*, similar collections are *Sahih Muslim, Sunan Abu Dawud, Jami Tirmidhi, Sahih al-Nasa'i,* and *Sunan Majah*. These collections not only supply the raw materials from which various Islamic laws are derived but provide the nuts and bolts of how Muslims are to live. These instructions from Muhammad include details on the performance of the worship rituals as well as mundane things like how to use the toilet. Imitation of Muhammad, in every detail, is the highest form of piety. Very few Muslims have actually read these volumes, but the contents of these volumes have permeated the Islamic community through a shared cultural tradition.

Shari'a

Shari'a is Islamic law. The term literally means "path," or "the right path," or "the path to the watering hole." *Shari'a* is comprehensive, covering every possible human action. Muslims consider it God's revealed legal system for humanity. When followed it will produce the most harmonious, just, fair and well-ordered society possible. Laws derived from human sources, such as legislatures and courts, are inferior to *shari'a* and therefore considered corrupt. The Islamic theological conception of unity, *tawhid*, means there is no separation between the sacred and the secular, religion and law or politics. For many Muslims, following *shari'a* is just as much an act of obedience to God as is ritual prayer.

Shari'a is derived from two primary sources and two secondary sources. The primary sources are, not surprisingly, the Qur'an and the *hadith*. What is surprising is the Qur'an contains so little legal material. Scholars identify only 350 to 500 verses in the Qur'an that can be described as legal, and most of those are extraordinarily vague. For instance, the Qur'an provides for contract law in these two verses:

> You who believe, fulfill your obligations. (5:1)

and

> You who believe, why do you say things and then not do them? (61:2)

The Qur'an on trusts and standards of judgment, provides only this:

> God commands you [people] to return things entrusted to you to their rightful owners, and, if you judge between people, to do so with justice: ... (4:58)

On business transactions and property law, the Qur'an says only this:

> You who believe, do not wrongfully consume each other's wealth but trade by mutual consent. (4:29)

On international relations, the Qur'an instructs the Muslim community as follows:

> He does not **forbid you** to deal kindly and justly with anyone who has not fought you for your faith or driven you out of your homes: (60:8, bold by the author)

On criminal law generally, the Qur'an provides the briefest instruction:

> Let harm be requited by an equal harm. (42:40)

All of this is innocent enough. But, when the Qur'an gets specific about criminal law, it raises the ire of both the non-Muslim and much of the Muslim world itself. The Qur'an outlines punishments for five specific crimes. These are known as the *hadd* punishments. The specified crimes are murder, theft, highway robbery, sexual misconduct, and slanderous accusation of sexual misconduct. The punishment for murder is the death penalty, unless the family of the victim forgives the accused and agrees to accept blood money. (The rule is for the murder of another Muslim. Murder of a non-Muslim carries only a financial penalty.) The punishment for theft is the amputation of the thief's hands, as the Qur'an provides:

> Cut off the hands of thieves, whether they are man or woman, as punishment for what they have done— a deterrent from God: God is almighty and wise. But if anyone repents after his wrongdoing and makes amends, God will accept his repentance: God is most forgiving, most merciful. (5:38-39)

There is significant disagreement among Islamic legal scholars over the application of the repentance clause. Generally speaking, one line of thinking is the thief's repentance earns him or her forgiveness in the next world, but does nothing to prevent the punishment of amputation in this world. The other line of thinking is the thief is allowed to repent and make amends *before he or she is caught.* In doing so, the thief avoids amputation. All the scholars agree that once caught, the amputation must take place.

Concerning highway robbery, punishments range from beheading, crucifixion, amputation of hands and feet on opposite sides, to banishment or imprisonment in the modern age. This depends on whether anyone was killed in the course of the robbery, whether there was murder without theft of property or only threats of either.

The punishment for sexual misconduct is one hundred lashes:

> Strike the adulteress and the adulterer one hundred times. Do not let compassion for them keep you from carrying out God's law—if you believe in God and the Last Day—and ensure that a group of believers witnesses the punishment. (24:2)

The punishment for slanderous allegation of sexual misconduct is eighty lashes. Other features of *shari'a* are particularly disturbing to non-Muslims. These include the death penalty for leaving Islam, *jihad,* and some of the rules regarding women.

The second primary source of *shari'a* is the *hadith.* This should not surprise us given the lack of legal material in the Qur'an, and the instruction to follow Muhammad's words and deeds. Whenever Muhammad speaks or acts on legal matters, Islam considers this a divine source of legislation. There are between 1200 and 5000 legal *hadiths.* These *hadiths* provide details and specification of the Qur'an's general principles. They also provide limitations on what would otherwise appear to be absolute rules in the Qur'an and explanation of the Qur'an's legal verses. The legal *hadiths* also address new matters not mentioned in the Qur'an. Islamic specialists acknowledge that most of *shari'a* derived from the Qur'an and *hadiths* carry forward pre-Islamic, pagan Arab conceptions and rules of law.

Where verses of the Qur'an and the *hadith* contradict one another, Islamic legal scholars developed the doctrine of *naskh,* or abrogation (cancellation). We have already seen one instance in the account of the Satanic Verses. Generally speaking, when two verses directly contradict one another, and the contradiction cannot be explained, the latter revealed Qur'an verse or later occurring *hadith* cancels the earlier. There is great disagreement among Islamic legal scholars concerning the precise number of times abrogation occurs, and with regard to which particular verses. Abrogation can result in the Qur'anic verse remaining in the text or being removed altogether.

Well-known examples of abrogation deal with alcoholic beverages and violence against non-Muslims. With regard to alcoholic beverages, the Qur'an first instructed Muslims not to come to prayers drunk. A later revelation said alcoholic drink contains some benefit and some detriment, but the detriment outweighs the benefit. Finally, the Qur'an forbade the drinking of alcoholic beverages altogether.

With regard to violence toward non-Muslims, a famous verse revealed during the Meccan period, when Muhammad was trying to attract converts, said:

> There is no compulsion in religion. (2:256)

However, the majority of Islamic legal scholars contend this verse was abrogated by a later verse revealed after Muhammad and the Muslims became more powerful. The abrogating verse is called the "Verse of the Sword":

> When the [four] forbidden months are over, wherever you encounter the idolaters, kill them, seize them, besiege them, wait for them at every lookout post; but if they turn [to God], maintain the prayer, and pay the prescribed alms, let them go on their way, for God is most forgiving and merciful. (9:5)

It is almost impossible to understand which verses have been abrogated. To fully understand this doctrine one must consult commentaries on the Qur'an or volumes on Islamic law.

The secondary sources of Islamic law are *ijma*, or "consensus" and *ijtihad*, which means "independent legal reasoning." *Ijma* is a source of *shari'a* when all the Muslim community, as represented by its learned jurists, agree on a matter at any given point in time. Once established, such matter is forever a part of *shari'a*. Experts disagree on whether *ijma* can be established with any certainty and disagree on exactly who must be a part of the consensus. In any event, matters established by *ijma* make up less than one percent of the overall body of *shari'a*.

Ijtihad is the process by which a qualified Muslim jurist strives to determine what the law is on the facts of the case before him when neither the text of the Qur'an or the *hadith*, nor *ijma*, address the issue. There are a number of "tools" at the disposal of the judge. These include drawing an analogy between known rules and the facts of the case to determine whether to extend the known law. Other "tools" include considerations of equity and the public interest, as well as the preference of the judge.

Over the first several hundred years of Islam, legal schools developed different understandings of the legal rules, including differing priorities for the various tools of *ijtihad*. The schools are known by the names of early prominent jurists, although the schools were significantly influenced by other scholars within the schools. The Sunni schools of *shari'a* are the Hanbali, Hanafi, Shafi'i, and Maliki. The most prominent Shi'ite school is the Jafari.

One may properly conclude that there is flexibility in *shari'a*. This is clear from the existence of several Islamic legal schools. Many of the tools of *ijtihad*, such as juristic preference and considerations of public interest, leave significant discretion to the judge. This flexibility theoretically allows for changes to accommodate the times and cultures of the various human communities. There is also a wide divergence of views within the Islamic community on the desirability of implementing *shari'a* as the law of the land in the first place.

One final note on *shari'a* as it relates to courts in the United States is worth mentioning. At the time of this writing, several state legislatures have introduced bills to prevent their courts from considering *shari'a*. In the view of this author, the bills are misplaced. Much of *shari'a* deals with the five pillars of Islam, i.e., the religious rituals, and are of no concern to non-Muslims. Most of the rest of *shari'a* deals with commercial transactions, wills, trusts, inheritance, family law matters, and other things that are likewise of little importance to non-Muslims. Most of *shari'a* in these areas was established by judges rather than by the text of the Qur'an and the *hadith*. These judges were seriously looking for the fairest and most just rules for the cases before them, much like common law courts do in the West. The only areas of *shari'a* that are of concern to both Muslims and non-Muslims alike are the *hadd* punishments, rules on apostasy, and some of the laws dealing with *jihad* and women's rights.

The courts of the United States must apply the statutory law of the U.S. and the particular state in which they operate. They must also apply the law previously determined by superior courts of their particular jurisdiction. Neither *shari'a* nor any other source of law may be considered. Thus, courts can never apply the criminal law of the Qur'an, nor its *hadd* penalties. These conflict with the statutory criminal law of the US and the individual states. Laws against apostasy violate our constitution. Qur'anic laws dealing with women's rights violate not only our statutory and common laws but our public policy as well. Thus, United States courts do not have the authority to consider or apply *shari'a* to cases before them.

As of this writing, no court in the United States has used *shari'a* as the controlling law of a case. Courts have enforced contracts, prenuptial agreements, and divorce decrees *where the parties themselves* agreed to the terms of their contracts with reference to the requirements of *shari'a*. Even then, the courts have never been called on to determine what is the law of *shari'a* or been asked (successfully) to apply *shari'a* to the case. Nor has any party been subjected to the imposition of *shari'a* as the controlling law of the case against their will. Although things can change, at this point, fear about *shari'a* making its way into American courts is unfounded.

CHAPTER 4

Contemporary Issues in Brief

Jihad

JIHAD MEANS "STRUGGLE" IN Arabic. In practice this means the use of violence to expand Islam. In modern times some have drawn a distinction between a so-called "greater jihad" and "lesser jihad". The "greater *jihad*" is said to be the internal struggle within Muslims to overcome their base instincts and become the best Muslims they can be. The traditional, or "lesser *jihad*", is the armed struggle against the enemies of Islam. This distinction, however, does not exist in the Qur'an, the hadith, shari'a, or traditional Islamic scholarship. We will be addressing only the traditional definition of jihad.

The Qur'an, the *hadith* and biographies of Muhammad are full of commands and examples of violence. A sample of the more than one hundred Qur'anic verses on fighting and violence are these:

> Fight in God's cause against those who fight you, ... Kill them wherever you encounter them, ... If they do fight you, kill them— this is what such disbelievers deserve— but if they stop, then God is most forgiving and merciful. Fight them until there is no more persecution, and worship is devoted to God. (2:190-193)
>
> Fighting is ordained for you, though you dislike it. You

may dislike something although it is good for you, or like something although it is bad for you: God knows and you do not. (2:216)

the disbelievers ... are your sworn enemies. (4:101)

Let those of you who are willing to trade the life of this world for the life to come, fight in God's way. To anyone who fights in God's way, whether killed or victorious, We shall give a great reward... The believers fight for God's cause, while those who reject faith fight for an unjust cause. Fight the allies of Satan: Satan's strategies are truly weak. (4:74-75)

They would dearly like you to reject faith, as they themselves have done, to be like them. So do not take them as allies until they migrate for God's cause. If they turn, then seize and kill them wherever you encounter them. Take none of them as an ally or supporter. (4:89, translator's editorial material removed by the author)

Those believers who stay at home, apart from those with an incapacity, are not equal to those who commit themselves and their possessions to striving [fighting] in God's way. God has raised such people to a rank above those who stay at home: ... (4:95, bracketed material added to reflect the terminology used in most English translations)

Your Lord revealed to the angels: 'I am with you: give the believers firmness; I shall put terror into the hearts of the disbelievers— strike above their necks and strike all their fingertips.' That was because they opposed God and His Messenger, and if anyone opposes God and His Messenger, God punishes them severely— 'That is what you get! Taste that!'—and the torment of the Fire awaits the disbelievers.

Believers, when you meet the disbelievers in battle, never turn your backs on them: if anyone does so on such a day— unless maneuvering to fight or to join a fighting group— he incurs the wrath of God, and Hell will be his home, a wretched destination! (8:12-16)

Let not the unbelievers think that they have got away and get the better (of the godly): they will never frustrate (them). Against them make ready your strength to the utmost of your power, including steeds of war, to strike terror into (the hearts of) the enemies, of Allah and your enemies, and others besides, whom ye may not know, but whom Allah doth know. (8:59-60, Yusuf Ali translation[16]) Prophet, urge the believers to fight: if there are twenty of you who are steadfast, they will overcome two hundred, and a hundred of you, if steadfast, will overcome a thousand of the disbelievers, for they are people who do not understand. (8:65)

… wherever you encounter the idolaters, kill them, seize them, besiege them, wait for them at every lookout post; but if they turn [to God], maintain the prayer, and pay the prescribed alms, let them go on their way, for God is most forgiving and merciful. (9:5)

Fight them: God will punish them at your hands, He will disgrace them, He will help you to conquer them … (9:14)

Fight those who believe not in Allah nor the Last Day, nor hold that forbidden which has been forbidden by Allah and His Messenger, nor acknowledge the religion of Truth, (even if they are) of the People of the Book [Christians and Jews], until they pay the jizya [tax on non-Muslims] with willing submission, and feel themselves subdued. (9:29, Yusuf Ali translation, bracketed material added by the author)

When you meet the disbelievers in battle, strike them in the neck, and once they are defeated, bind any captives firmly … He will not let the deeds of those who are killed for His cause come to nothing. (47:4)

God truly loves those who fight in solid lines for His cause, like a well-compacted wall. (61:4)

We have also seen that as soon as Muhammad migrated to Medina and had at his disposal fighting men, he led them on raids of Meccan caravans and regional tribes. Such attacks and raids continued, as the revelations

---

16   Abdullah Yusuf Ali, *The Holy Qur'an* (New Delhi: Goodword, 2003).

cited above came down, throughout the rest of Muhammad's life. After his death, Abu Bakr led the Muslims in the Wars of Apostasy to conquer the Arabian Peninsula. The Muslim forces continued northward and did not stop until defending armies defeated them. The violent nature of Islam is obvious on its face.

However, most Muslims in the world are peace-loving, hospitable people. How do we account for this? There are a number of answers, some of which overlap. First, most Muslims have never read the Qur'an and simply don't know its teachings on violence and *jihad*. These Muslims have little or no knowledge of the history of Muhammad and the Muslims in Medina, the Wars of Apostasy, or the conquests of the Persians and Byzantines. They have been taught only bits and pieces of Islam, usually from their parents or other elder family members.

Those more knowledgeable offer various explanations. Some argue the Muslims never attacked anyone, but only defended themselves or attacked those who were preparing to launch an attack against them. Or, they say in the early days of Islam, the Muslims had to fight to establish a safe base of support for the religion. Given the success and stability of Islam, the commands to fight do not apply anymore. Others say all of the commands to fight are defensive in nature. Others say the commands to fight are defensive but apply only when the Muslim community is under attack for reasons of religion alone. Regardless of the argument, the end result is the violence and *jihad* verses only applied during the early years of Islam, or apply in rare or extraordinary circumstances. They have no relevance to Islam today.

Yet, we see Muslim terrorists at work. They desire to kill as many people as they can and rely on the text of the Qur'an for justification of their actions. The terrorists, sometimes referred to as *jihadis* or militant *salafis*, believe they are obeying God's commands in the Qur'an. They take the verses quoted previously, and other verses, as universal commands to all Muslims. We will now take a brief and very simplistic look at the terrorists.

During the early decades of the twentieth century, Muslim observers pondered the state of the Islamic world compared to the West. Islam was backward economically, educationally, technologically, and in most every other measure. The challenge was to explain this state of affairs given that Islam is God's only religion and obedience thereto guarantees the best possible human society. They determined that Muslims had abandoned true Islam and were living an Islam mixed with *bida*, or "innovation," including all sorts of non-Islamic beliefs and ideals. The answer for the Muslim world was to follow a pure Islam, an Islam like that of the first three generations of Muslims. These first three generations are called the "righteous ancestors" or *salafs*. Those who propose this purification are called *salafis*.

Salafism encompasses a large number of divergent groups. Some *salafis* contend the purification needed is simply to remove from the Muslim world all western influences. Others believe the *salafs* were also demonstrably violent, attacking non-believers in an effort to take Islam to the four corners of the earth. As long as the *salafs* were faithful to a pure Islam, they were successful. Their armed advance only stalled when these Muslims abandoned the pure Islam of their earlier days. Thus, these *salafis* see violence as not only a means to the objective of installing Islam as the world's one true religion, but as necessary if one seeks to be a true, faithful Muslim. In other words, *jihad* is a pillar of Islam.

The goal of these *jihadis* is first to recreate the Islamic caliphate. The recreated caliphate would control the territory held by the last caliphate, the Ottoman Empire. Once the caliphate is re-established, and *shari'a* is the law of the land, Islam will shine forth as the supreme belief system and the Muslim community will appear as the best on earth. In the meantime, they view the fractured collection of Muslim nation-states as a tool of the pagan Europeans to keep the Muslims weak and divided. The various Muslim nations must be reunited. This means those kings and dictators who rule these countries must be removed, and legitimate Islamic rulers committed to the caliphate must be installed. Israel is a huge problem being squarely in the middle of this future caliphate.

Jihadis believe the support of the United States military has prevented success in overthrowing these kings and dictators. Before having the opportunity to overthrow these regimes, the US military must be driven from the region. Thus, terrorism is a tool to drive out the US from the lands of the caliphate. If attacks directly against the military are not likely to be successful, then attacks against American civilians will make the price of staying in the region too high for the American public to stomach.

The Arab Spring of 2012 was a remarkable gift to these militant *salafis*. What could not be accomplished through direct, violent means has happened by popular uprising. Generally speaking, these uprisings were not carried out by the *jihadis* or their sympathizers, but were carried out by common people who desired to throw off oppressive dictators. However, once the kings and dictators were gone, the most organized opposition stepped into the power vacuum. That organized opposition was usually the *jihadi* parties. We have already seen the Muslim Brotherhood take control of Egypt, if only temporarily. We will see what the future holds in the Middle East and in other Muslim-majority regions in the coming decades.

Women's Rights

There are different perspectives on the status of women in Islam. Muslims will assert that Muhammad was the world's first great liberator and advocate of women's rights. This perspective might be justified if one looks at the rights of women under Islam compared with the rights of women in pre-Islamic, pagan Arab society. Muhammad did improve the lot of women in some respects. The most widely-cited instance of this was Islam's prohibition of female infanticide. In times of drought or other severe hardship, the nomadic tribes would bury their newborn daughters in the desert sands. They did this to avoid seeing their daughters slowly starve to death or to avoid the possibility of seeing them turn to prostitution later in life in order to survive.

Muhammad eliminated this practice with the following revelation:

> When one of them is given news of the birth of a baby girl, his face darkens and he is filled with gloom. In his shame he hides himself away from his people because of the bad news he has been given. Should he keep her and suffer contempt or bury her in the dust? How ill they judge! (16:58-5)

Although there is some debate about exactly how bad pre-Islamic conditions were for women, it is generally thought they had little or no legal status, and were considered nothing but chattel. From a base line of no rights at all, Islam represented a significant improvement. Islam gave women the right to inherit, the right to testify, and the right to certain limits in the physical violence a husband could visit upon his wife. Polygamy was limited to four wives at any one time. Men were not to marry orphans in order to obtain their property. And there were general exhortations to justice and fairness.

However, from the perspective of modernity, especially in the West, Islam has institutionalized women as second-class citizens and resulted in widespread physical and emotional abuse by men. Since Muslims see the Islamic texts as the revealed will of God, they are above reproach. Islam thus creates an iron-clad paternalistic society.

Islam provides that Muslim men may marry up to four wives at a time, but gives women no right beyond one husband:

> If you fear that you will not deal fairly with orphan girls, you may marry whichever [other] women seem good to you, two, three, or four. If you fear that you cannot be equitable [to them], then marry only one, or your slave(s): ... (4:3)

Islam allows men to beat wives from whom they fear disobedience but gives wives no such right to beat husbands:

> If you fear high-handedness from your wives, remind them [of the teachings of God], then ignore them when you go to bed, then hit them. (4:34)

Other English translations of this verse use the word "beat" instead of "hit." (See the translations of Yusuf Ali, Shakir and Muhsin Khan). Some Muslim apologists try to soften the impact of this instruction to physical abuse of wives claiming the husband can only softly tap her or something similar. Outside the prying eyes of Westerners, Muslim scholars instruct their flocks that the husband must only avoid the face and not break bones or draw blood.

Muslim men may marry pre-pubescent girls. This is apparent from the Quran's instructions concerning divorce. The following passage describes the waiting period after a man divorces his wife. The waiting period is designed to allow a pregnancy to become apparent if conception occurred in the last days before the divorce. If so, a husband may revoke the divorce.

[The] period of waiting will be three months for those women who have ceased menstruating and for those who have not [yet] menstruated; the waiting period of those who are pregnant will be until they deliver their burden: ...(65:4)[17]

In fact, Muhammad's marriage to Aisha confirms that pre-pubescent girls were fair game to Muslim men. Aisha, the daughter of Abu Bakr, was only six years old when Muhammad married her. He waited until she was nine years old before consummating the marriage.[18]

According to the Qur'an, women inherit half what a man inherits:

Concerning your children, God commands you that a son should have the equivalent share of two daughters. (4:11)

Likewise, a woman's testimony is worth half that of a man's:

Call in two men as witnesses. If two men are not there, then call one man and two women out of those you approve as witnesses, so that if one of the two women should forget the other can remind her. (2:282)

Muhammad explained this by instructing that women are inferior to men both spiritually and intellectually. Muhammad said, "This is because of the deficiency of the woman's mind."[19] He also said, "This is the deficiency in her religion."[20] He also taught a group of women as follows: "O womenfolk, you should ask for forgiveness for I saw you in bulk

---

17   Taken with Qur'an 33:49, which says no waiting period is necessary for marriages that were not consummated, this verse provides that men may marry and have sex with pre-pubescent girls. For confirmation of this interpretation, please see *Asbab al-Nuzul* ("Reasons for the Revelations") of al-Wahidi, and the *Tafsirs* ("Commentaries on the Qur'an") of Jalalayn, ibn Kathir, ibn Abbas, Mawdudi and Qutb, among others.

18   *Sahih Bukhari* 58:234, 236; 62:64, 65, 88; *Sahih Muslim* 8:3309, 3310, 3311; 41:4915

19   *Sahih Bukhari* 48:826

20   *Sahih Bukhari* 6:301

amongst the dwellers of Hell. A wise lady said: Why is it, Allah's Apostle, that women comprise the bulk of the inhabitants of Hell? The Prophet observed: 'You curse too much and are ungrateful to your spouses. You lack common sense, fail in religion and rob the wisdom of the wise.' Upon this the woman remarked: What is wrong with our common sense? The Prophet replied, 'Your lack of common sense can be determined from the fact that the evidence of two women is equal to one man. That is a proof."[21]

Muhammad also said women are an evil omen,[22] that married men should never trust their wives,[23] and that women are the most harmful affliction to men.[24] We have already seen that menstruating women are unclean, that their prayers are void, and that a woman walking between a man and the *qibla* voids his prayer.

The Qur'an also allows Muslim men to rape their slave girls, and rape newly captured women, even if they are already married, and even with their husbands present.

> Man was truly created anxious: ... Not so those who pray... who guard their chastity from all but their spouses or their slave-girls—there is no blame attached to [relations with] these,... (70:19-20)
> Do not marry women that your fathers married ... women already married, other than your slaves. (4:22 and 24)
> "Abu Sa'id al-Khudri (Allah her pleased with him) reported that at the Battle of Hanain Allah's Messenger (may peace be upon him) sent an army to Autas and encountered the enemy and fought with them. Having overcome them and taken them captives, the Companions of Allah's Messenger (may peace be upon him) seemed to refrain from having intercourse with captive women because of their husbands being polytheists. Then Allah, Most High, sent down regarding that: "And women already married, except those whom your right hands possess (4: 24)" (i. e.

---

21 *Sahih Muslim* 1:142

22 *Sahih Bukhari* 52:110

23 Ibn Ishaq, *The Life of Muhammad*, translated by Alfred Guillaume (Oxford: Oxford University Press, 1955), page 584.

24 *Sahih Bukhari* 62:33

they were lawful for them when their 'Idda period came
to an end).[25]

Much more could be said on the subject of Islam and women, but these
passages illustrate the point.

Folk Beliefs

As Islam spread, both in the early decades of the conquests and later
through missionary efforts in the Far East, converts accepted the unity of
God, the prophethood of Muhammad, and the authority of the Qur'an.
However, Islam did not replace the traditional beliefs of the converts but
cast a veneer over those beliefs. Thus, Muslims around the world adhere
not only to orthodox Islamic doctrine but to a large variety of superstitious
beliefs.

These folk beliefs include beliefs in spells, curses, incantations, amulets,
warding off evil spirits and attracting blessings, or"*baraka*". Muslims wear
tiny Qur'ans around their necks to protect against evil spirits, recite the
confession of faith or various passages of the Qur'an for good luck, or
seek the advice and counsel of various spiritual guides. Orthodox Muslim
scholars renounce all of these practices as foreign to Islam. Yet some of
these beliefs and practices are rooted in the Qur'an and the *hadith*.

One of the most widely-held superstitious beliefs in the Muslim world
is the belief in the "evil eye." The evil eye is a curse unleashed when someone
envies something another owns. The envy unleashes the curse, and the
curse brings harm, damage or loss to the thing envied. Thus, whenever
complimenting a person's home, car or children, one should follow the
compliment with the Arabic phrase *mashallah*. This literally means "it is
God's will for you" but serves to protect the item or person from the curse
of the evil eye. An amulet commonplace in Turkey and often seen in other
Muslim countries is round and blue, with a smaller white circle in the
middle, and a black dot within the white circle. This amulet is made into a
piece of jewelry or a picture frame and placed over doorways or hung from
rearview mirrors. The amulet serves to protect against the evil eye.

---

25 *Sahih Muslim* 8:3432. *Sunan Abu Dawud* 2:2150 – "... in the presence of their
husbands ..."

Is there support for the curse of the evil eye and other superstitious beliefs in the Qur'an? *Sura* 113, the next to last *sura* of the Qur'an, reads as follows:

> Say [Prophet], 'I seek refuge with the Lord of daybreak against the harm in what He has created, the harm in the night when darkness gathers, the harm in witches when they blow on knots, the harm in the envier when he envies.' (113:15)

Here, God tells Muhammad to seek refuge with Him from "the envier when he envies." This verse seems to admit the curse of the "evil eye" is an actual curse from which Muhammad should seek refuge with God.

Sura 113 also advises Muhammad to seek refuge from the power of witches. The reason for the verse "the harm in witches when they blow on knots" is given in al-Wahidi's "Reasons for the Revelations."

> "The Messenger of Allah, Allah bless him and give him peace, had a Jewish servant boy. The Jews approached him and kept after him until he gave them some fallen hair from the Prophet, Allah bless him and give him peace, as well as a few teeth from his comb. The Jews used these to cast a spell of black magic on him. The person who was behind this was the Jew Labid ibn al-A'sam. He then put the hair in a well belonging to Banu Zurayq called Dharwan. The Messenger of Allah, Allah bless him and give him peace, fell ill for a period of six month, during which the hair of his head fell off; he imagined that he slept with his wives when he did not, and was withering away without knowing the reason. As he was one day sleeping, he saw two angels coming to him. One of them sat at his head and the other at his feet. The angel who sat at his head asked: 'What is wrong with the man?' The second angel responded: 'A spell of black magic was cast on him'. The first one asked: 'And who is responsible for this sorcery?' The second angel answered: 'It is Labid ibn al-A'sam, the Jew'. The first angel asked again: 'What did he use to cast black magic on him?' The second angel said: 'He used a

comb and fallen hair'. The first angel asked: 'Where is it now?' The second angel said: 'It is inside the spadix of a palm tree beneath the stepping stone which is inside the well of Dharwan', at which point the Messenger of Allah, Allah bless him and give him peace, woke up. He said: 'O 'A'ishah, do you not think that this is from Allah to inform me of the cause of my illness?' He then sent 'Ali [ibn Abi Talib], al-Zubayr [ibn al-'Awwam] and 'Ammar [ibn Yasir] who drained the water of that well as one would drain the dust of henna. They lifted the stone and got the spadix out and found therein some of the hair of the Messenger of Allah, Allah bless him and give him peace, as well a few teeth from his comb. They also found with it a string with eleven knots knitted with needles. Allah, exalted is He, then revealed Surah al-Falaq [Sura 113] and Surah al-Nas (al-Mu'awwidhatayn). With each verse that the Messenger of Allah, Allah bless him and give him peace, read one knot was untied and the Prophet, Allah bless him and give him peace, felt some lightness. When the last knot was untied, the Prophet, Allah bless him and give him peace, got up as if he was released from a cord to which he was tied up. Gabriel, peace be upon him, kept saying: 'In the name of Allah I cast this incantation on you to protect you from anything that might harm you and that Allah heals you from the resentful envier and the evil eye'.[26]

Thus, we see *sura* 113 was revealed as a cure from a spell placed upon Muhammad by black magic and a protection from the curse of the evil eye. The commentary on *sura* 113 provided by Ibn Kathir provides additional information on the prevalent belief of Muhammad in the reality of these spells, curses, black magic, and the evil eye.[27] Muslims who believe in

---

26   Al-Wahidi, *Asbab al-Nuzul* ("Reasons for the Revelations'), commentary on *sura* 113, found at http://www.altafsir.com/AsbabAlnuzol.asp?SoraName=113&Ayah =0&search=yes&img=A, accessed December 19, 2012. Bracketed material added by the author.

27   See Ibn Kathir at http://www.quran4u.com/Tafsir%20Ibn%20Kathir/PDF/113-114%20falaq,%20Nas.pdf, accessed December 19, 2012.

these things and make them a regular part of their daily spiritual existence are following the example of their prophet and the Qur'an, as they are commanded to do.

Modernity

We have seen the efforts made by moderate Muslims to avoid treating the Qur'an's commands to violence as applicable in the modern age. Muslims accomplish this by treating the "violence verses" as having been limited to the specific context of seventh-century Arabia, or to very narrowly defined parameters that are unlikely to arise in the modern age.

Moderate Muslims treat the "misogynist verses," those verses that abuse women and treat them as inferior to men, in the same way they treat the violence verses. Muslims say the culture of Muhammad's time was so backward and primitive that only incremental improvement in the lives of women was likely to take hold. General principles of fairness and justice, while not applied to women at the time, are nevertheless the overriding considerations. Since equal treatment of women in the modern world is possible, it should be done.

Such is the explanation usually offered or understood by many Muslims. Moderate scholars offer more subtle rationales. Mahmoud Mohamed Taha said the Islam of Mecca was the true Islam. This Islam taught tolerance, respect and affirmation of other faiths, advocacy of human rights, etc. This was the Islam Allah intended. When the people rejected the Islam preached by Muhammad in Mecca, they demonstrated they were not advanced enough to embrace it. Allah retreated to a more primitive version of Islam, the Islam revealed in Medina. Since humanity is now well-prepared for the true Islam of Mecca, it must reject the Islam of Medina. This includes rejection of violence, the oppression of women and non-Muslims, and the exacting legal rules of Shari'a.[28]

Irshad Manji explains the ugly aspects of Islam as the embodiment of the culture and thinking of desert nomads of seventh-century Arabia. She describes Islam as being pulled between the universal values of tolerance, human rights, respect for others, equal rights for the genders, etc. which constitute the true Islam, and the "hoary tribalism" of the violent and

---

28   Mahmoud Mohamed Taha, *The Second Message of Islam*. Translated by Abdullahi Ahmed an-Na'im (Syracuse, NY: Syracuse University Press, 1987)

misogynist culture in which Islam was revealed. Her answer for Islam moving forward is to reject the Arab tribalism in all its forms, and embrace the universal values Islam shares with so many other faiths.[29]

Contrasted with these and other moderate Muslim voices are the voices of the fundamentalists. The fundamentalists preach that true Islam constitutes adherence and obedience to the literal text of the Qur'an, imitation of Muhammad in every respect, and full implementation of *shari'a* as the only law of the land. The moderates and fundamentalists continue to wage this battle of ideas for the heart and future of Islam. The outcome of this battle will undoubtedly impact the future of our world to a very significant degree.

---

29 Irshad Manji, *The Trouble with Islam Today: A Muslim's Call for Reform in Her Faith* (New York: St. Martin's Griffin, 2003).

Action Item Checklist

Part 1: *Islam and Muslims*

- ☐ Understand the Basics of Islamic History, Belief, and Theology
- ☐ Identify the Five Pillars of Islamic Practice
- ☐ Familiarize Yourself with the Qur'an, the Hadith and Shari'a
- ☐ Develop a Compassionate Heart for Muslims Rather than One of Fear or Suspicion

It is imperative to never use what you have learned in Part 1 as a basis for attacks against Islam or Muslims. Respect Muslims as people and treat them as equals. Remember that most Muslims are unaware of the history of Islam and even what the Qur'an says. Attacking another person's beliefs is never helpful.

PART TWO
MINISTERING THE GOSPEL TO MUSLIMS

CHAPTER 5
Relationships with Muslims

Muslims Are Not "Objects" of Ministry

GOD LOVES MUSLIMS. HE loves them with the same everlasting love with which he loves everyone else. When Jesus was being beaten, spit upon and humiliated, His compassionate heart was bleeding for Muslims. When Jesus died on the cross, he died for Muslims. God's love for them is not conditional, just like it is not for anyone else. God will go on loving them throughout eternity whether they turn and cry out to Jesus or not.

Since we are to love others as God loves us, we must have the same compassionate heart for Muslims that God has for them. This means that they must never become "objects" of ministry. Our ministry to them cannot be a box to check on a list. It cannot be a method of demonstrating our spirituality. It cannot be a "thing to do." We must never view Muslims as prizes or trophies, or medals won in a spiritual battle. They are real people. They face the same struggles, the same fears, the same hurts and disappointments we all face. We must look beyond their identity as Muslims and see real people – each one precious to Jesus.

Before embarking on ministry to Muslims, we must examine our hearts. Are we motivated by compassion? Do we have a sense of Godly respect for them? Do we value them as fellow travelers in life or look down upon them in some way? Are we willing to be genuine friends who are loyal and faithful no matter what? Are we willing to invest our hearts in selfless service to them regardless of whether they ever come to faith?

If we wrestle with these questions and honestly answer "yes" to each one, then we will dispense with "relationship evangelism." Too often, this concept carries with it negative implications. We tend to view relationship evangelism as a tool by which we "earn the right" to share the gospel with someone. Once we have shared the gospel, if we do not get the response we want the relationship ends and we move on. This constitutes nothing more than acting as though we love, respect and value a person when in reality we have a hidden agenda. We represent ourselves in a false way. This is not holiness and godliness. This is manipulation.

We must come to see that Jesus calls us to live out the whole character of God. Sharing the truth of the gospel is only one aspect of this whole. There is genuine kingdom value in giving a cup of cold water to a thirsty person, in feeding the hungry, in crying with a widow, in comforting hurting people, in encouraging those who are down, in accepting the unlovable and in embracing the rejected. The world should see these things as characterizing all aspects of our lives, not only that slice of our lives we designate as "ministry." This kind of Christ-like love, sacrifice, service and loyalty creates the environment whereby the truth of the gospel flows naturally. It becomes an overflow of who we are rather than the fulfillment of a religious duty.

Initial Encounters

"I don't think I've ever seen a Muslim."

Despite living in the seventh largest city in the United States, I have heard this said more than a few times. For those who live in rural America and rarely travel to "the city," this could be true. For the rest of us, this is probably an illusion. Why would people think they've never seen a Muslim? Those who have attempted to estimate the number of Muslims in the United States have arrived at figures between two and ten million. Muslims live in significant numbers in every major and medium-sized American city, and at least a few Muslims live in almost every smaller city across the country.

One reason most Americans seemingly never encounter Muslims is they are simply not paying attention. We all have busy lives and we rush from one place to another attempting to accomplish our "list of things to do." We often don't pay attention to the people we encounter and may only notice them to the extent they either help or hinder us in accomplishing the task at hand. Muslims move into and out of our daily experience like ghosts - there for a moment but indistinguishable from the mass of humanity.

A few years ago, when my older daughter approached sixteen years of age, she broached the subject of getting a car. She knew we had purchased a vehicle for her brother when he got his license, and now it was her turn. I asked her the following question.

"I'm not making any promises, but if you could have any car you wanted, within reason, of course, what would it be?"

"Well, I'd really like a blue Jeep Liberty," she said.

"Oh, I see you've thought about this. You even know the color you want."

"Yeah, I don't know if they make a blue one. I don't think I've ever seen one. Jeep Liberty is a very uncommon car. I hardly ever see them. So it might not be possible to find a blue one," she allowed.

"OK, I'll see what we can do."

At the Christmas following her sixteenth birthday, she received a several-year-old blue Jeep Liberty. Once she drove it around a while, an interesting thing happened. She said, "Dad, it's funny. I don't think I ever saw a blue Jeep Liberty until I got mine. Now I see them everywhere!"

This story reminds us that if we hope to impact the Muslim world for Christ, we have to start paying attention to the people we encounter in our daily lives. Whether Muslim or not, we have an opportunity to spread God's love in almost every encounter we have with others. If nothing else, we can look them in the eye, greet them, use their name and ask them about their day. The least we can do is thank them for their work and say "God bless you."

We can also begin to "tune our radar to the Muslim station." By this I mean keep our eyes and ears open for signs that the person we are encountering might be Muslim. How do we recognize a Muslim? Sometimes it is easy to recognize them, but other times not so easy. The easiest way to recognize them is if they happen to be wearing Muslim attire. If they live in an area where there is a significant Muslim presence, they are more likely to feel more comfortable wearing the clothing of their homeland. There is great variety in what that clothing might look like, and in many cases there is nothing about it that distinguishes it as Muslim. But if you encounter Arabs from the Arabian Peninsula, the loose-fitting black or white robes are a dead giveaway. Sometimes you will see a male dressed in a completely western manner with a woman who is covered with a scarf and a long dress. These are probably Muslims too. But most Muslims you encounter will not be distinguishable by clothing, so we need to have other ways to identify them.

Another way to them is by their name. Muslim parents very often use Islamic names for their children, and these names are easily identifiable. I would recommend an internet search of "most common Muslim boy names" and "most common Muslim girl names" in order to become familiar with them. However, some may change their given names from Muslim ones to western ones. Some of my closest friends have unofficially changed their first names to David, Matthew, and Ted. Unfortunately, they feel this is necessary to avoid receiving negative attention from those they encounter.

It can be very difficult to identify a Muslim by their appearance. A while back a friend of mine named Francisco walked into a local Arab grocery store. The store proprietor greeted him warmly.

"Ahlan wa sahlan, akhi. Kayfa haluka?"

Francisco replied, "I'm sorry, I don't speak Arabic."

"That's OK, brother. We can speak English. Say, brother. Where are you from?"

"I'm from Mexico."

"Oh, yes, yes. But where are you from originally?"

Francisco replied, "I'm from Mexico City."

"But where is your father from?"

"He's from Mexico City too. We are Mexicans."

Crest-fallen, the proprietor mumbled, "OK, well then, welcome."

This encounter teaches us something important about Arab Muslims, as well as about Latinos. They often resemble each other very closely. There are very good reasons for this. In the early eighth century, Muslims from North Africa, the "Moors," entered Spain at Gibraltar and conquered a large part of it for Islam. The name "Gibraltar" comes from the name of the Muslim general Tariq. "Tariq's hill" in Arabic is "Jabal Tariq" which morphed into "Gibraltar." The Muslim armies continued north into France until turned away at Tours by the forces of Charles Martel. The Muslims retreated to Spain, where they remained for almost eight centuries. Over these centuries, the Spanish intermarried with the Muslims, spoke Arabic, read Arabic literature, dressed in the Arab way, and some converted to

Islam. Even today, the sounds of traditional Arab guitar and Spanish Flamenco guitar are remarkably similar. Spanish and North African architectural features are also quite similar. The Spanish language adopted approximately 5000 Arabic words. The Moors remained in Spain until Ferdinand and Isabella drove them out in the year 1492, when Columbus sailed the ocean blue and brought this cultural, linguistic, and genetic mix to the new world. No wonder the Arab grocer mistook Francisco for an Arab Muslim. They might have been related!

The history summarized above is somewhat unhappily memorialized in the name of a city on the Texas-Mexico border across from Brownsville, Texas. The city is Matamoros, which is named for a Spanish general whose name means "death to the Moors".

There are two points to draw from this. First, we may encounter Arab and other Muslims and mistake them for Hispanics. Second, there is no Muslim "look." Muslims may resemble Hispanics, but they can also be African, Indian, Oriental, Anglo, or any other ethnicity. Muslims are found in most countries in the world, and in most ethnic groups. So in most cases we need to wrestle up a little more courage and actually talk to the people around us.

A simple way to identify a Muslim is to greet the person with the word "salaam." This is a universal greeting among Muslims, no matter what their native language. It is a shortened form of "as-salaamu alaykum" which means "peace be upon you." It is usually pronounced like "slam" with a short "a" added between the S and L.

When you greet someone with "salaam," you will likely get one of two responses. First, the person might tilt their head to one side and look at you strangely. This is a sure sign they are not a Muslim. The second response you might get is raised eyebrows, a smile or other surprised look, and a reply of "wa alaykum as-salaam. Are you Muslim?" Your response might be something like "No, but I thought you might be. Where are you from?"

At first, you might get an answer that identifies a region, such as "the Middle East" or "Asia" or even "Persia." (Persia is code for Iran.) This answer indicates a fear of a negative response, which unfortunately, they may be accustomed to when mentioning their actual home country. I suggest saying something like, "Well I figured (whatever region they named), but which country?" No matter what country they are from, make sure your response is positive. Raise your eyebrows and say something to indicate you find his or her country interesting, or fascinating, or note that it has been in the news, or express sadness if the news has been bad. The main point here is to distinguish yourself from so many others that respond with ambivalence, scorn, or worse. You want to be the opposite of those whose attitude is that foreigners should go back home. If you do this, you will appear intelligent, tolerant, open-minded, warm and friendly – exactly who you are!

At this point, you should assess your situation and decide whether additional conversation is warranted. If you are standing in some kind of retail service line, and there are people behind you, it might be better to move along. If so, make sure you have the person's name, note where you met them and the day and time you were there. Then, plan to return to that location at the same day and time, hoping to run into your new Muslim acquaintance again. You hope to have repeated encounters with them so you can deepen the friendship.

It is always good to ask questions about family. If your Muslim friend is in the United States alone, you should empathize with the emotions they probably feel, that being pain at missing their family. If they are here with their family, you can rejoice with them that they have their family with them. I should note here that you will need to be discerning, and not make assumptions about the person. Muslims are like anyone else. They are highly varied in education, lifestyle, income level, religious sentiment, and in any number of other ways. The point is you want to treat them like you would any other person with whom you are trying to develop a relationship. Try to connect with them early in the relationship in a way that reflects a sensitive and compassionate heart, a heart like Jesus. They most likely have never experienced a person like this before, and it should make a positive impression on them.

Where are we more likely to meet Muslims? My first suggestion would be to check the yellow pages for Arabic, Persian, or even Mediterranean restaurants. Look for Middle Eastern groceries. Hookah bars are trendy. Find mosques. Not only will you meet Muslims in these venues, their owners will usually locate these businesses where Muslims congregate. If you are a male and at all athletic, try municipal or school soccer fields. Muslim men often gather to play soccer on nights and weekends. I show up and act like I know what I am doing. If you don't play soccer, insist on playing fullback. In soccer, it is easier to mess up an opponent's scoring opportunity than create one for your team!

Your local denominational association office might have demographic information showing where various nationalities and ethnicities congregate in your city. Humanitarian aid agencies working with recent immigrants and refugees will likely have information on the national background of those they serve. They might not have a category for "Muslim," but they will almost certainly have information on nationality. Ask about persons from a country you have previously identified as Muslim-majority, and offer to help the agency serve the people from that country. If they ask why you are interested in that particular nationality, tell them you have a special place in your heart for people from that particular country, and would like to help them in any way you can. Most often, immigrants and refugees need help learning English. Their children will need tutoring with school work. They might need transportation to and from government offices and medical facilities.

Once you establish a "working" relationship with a family or group of refugees, you will have the opportunity to visit them in their homes. This will honor them, and indicate you value them as friends rather than as simply people who have particular needs you are able to meet. Take special care to treat them as equals. Throughout the process of relocating to a new and strange country, most refugees are treated as poor, inferior people who are at the mercy of the governmental or aid workers who attend to them. It will often seem a "breath of fresh air" not to be treated as objects of service. We are happy to serve them, but as equals who are capable of serving and blessing us in return.

There are more opportunities to serve Muslim refugees than you have time to serve. It is easy to get overwhelmed. Suggest to your Sunday school class, Bible study, church or fellowship that they adopt a particular group of Muslim refugees. This can be a very rewarding and spiritually significant ministry, and helps spread the workload among a number of people.

Deepening the Relationship

Our goal is to deepen our relationships with our new Muslim friends. Before we go further in our discussion, a word of warning about gender is warranted. In some Muslim contexts, unrelated men and women do not even look each other in the eye. It can be offensive for a man to speak to an unrelated female without first establishing a relationship with her husband or father. In some contexts, unrelated men and women are segregated, and friendships are limited to those of the same gender. As we pursue relationships with Muslims, males should not pursue friendships with females and vice versa. If you meet a Muslim of the opposite gender, make sure to introduce them to either your spouse or a friend who might also be involved in ministry to Muslims with you. We want to remove any doubt about hidden agendas right from the beginning. As time goes by, we may be able to establish a friendship with a Muslim of the opposite gender. It will most likely occur in the context of a relationship with a married couple or an entire family.

Let's move to the next step in the relationship-building process. Unless your new Muslim friend has been in the West for a long time and adopted Western cultural norms, he or she will expect that friends meet together for meals in homes. (This was also true in the West not so very long ago.) Thus, we will want to invite our new Muslim friend and his or her family to our home for a meal. They might invite you to their home first, and if so, you are ahead in the game. Accept their offer, and then expect to reciprocate within a couple of weeks.

Entertaining Muslims in your home, or vice versa, will open up the world of cultural norms and expectations. We need to be sensitive to these cultural factors to avoid causing offense. It may be that your new friends have lived in the West for decades, or are world travelers. In that case they may be familiar and comfortable with Western cultural practices. If this is the case, then much of the discussion below can be ignored. However, they may have only recently arrived in the West from a conservative Muslim environment, or may be struggling to maintain their own culture in a new land. In this case, these cultural factors may be very important. Until we know for sure, it is better to start with the most conservative position. It is easier to start conservatively and then move to a more lenient position than it is to undo damage done by violating a cultural expectation. With that in mind, let us consider some of the cultural factors that may come into play when dining in a home with our new Muslim friends.

Formality

If you are hosting dinner, prepare a formal affair. In the West, it is not uncommon for a host to say to a guest, "Make yourself at home." We value treatment of guests as family members and want them to feel as comfortable as they would in their own home. This will likely be offensive to Muslims and others from the East. Rather than a host honoring the guest by inviting him to dinner, in many Muslim countries, a guest honors the host by coming to the host's home for dinner. Thus, if the guest is honoring the host, the host will want to reciprocate that honor by serving a nice meal, prepared in the home, on matching place settings with silverware instead of plastic wear and the like. The hosts should dress more formally, as though they are going out for a dinner at an expensive restaurant. In short, do everything as though you are hosting dignitaries. You want to communicate by formality the importance you attach to the visit by your guests.

What Not to Serve

Whatever you do, do *not* serve pork, or any food that might have traces of pork in it. Pork is not only prohibited in Islam, it is detested. Conservative Muslims may be hesitant to accept your offer of dinner in your home for fear that you might either serve pork, might have cooked pork at some time in the recent past, or even that you might have had pork in your kitchen or refrigerator at any time in the past. If you sense any hesitation at your invitation, you can assure your guest that your home is *halal*. This means there is nothing un-Islamic in your kitchen, whether pork or alcohol.[30] Make sure you have just told the truth! Remove any pork product and any alcoholic beverage from your home. If need be, have friends store these items for you overnight.

Dogs

With apologies to all dog lovers, I regret to inform you that dogs are considered unclean in Islam. This does not mean literally dirty. It means that touching a dog defiles a Muslim, requiring him or her to perform *wudu*, or the ceremonial washing we discussed previously, before God will

---

30 Technically, any meat not sacrificed according to Islamic regulation is *haram*, or prohibited, the opposite of *halal*. But the Muslim is likely to assume you don't know that much about Islamic law, and are simply referring to pork. If they are very conservative, and still worried, you might gently and respectfully offer to go to their home instead.

accept their prayers. This belief results in conservative Muslims avoiding dogs at all cost. If you have a dog, the first option would be to keep the dog off premise by either having a neighbor keep the dog for the night or placing it in a kennel. The second option would be to kennel the dog in the garage or back yard, so long as it won't bark and remind your guests that your dog was probably only moments before lying on the very place they are now sitting. If your dog is a barker, go with option one.

Gender Boundaries

When your Muslim friends arrive at your home, pay attention to gender boundaries. Men should not greet the Muslim woman with an offer of a handshake. In conservative Muslim settings, there should never be any physical contact between unrelated men and women. For example, when my family and I lived in the Middle East, I once asked a Muslim friend about this rule. I proposed a hypothetical. "What if a woman falls while walking down the street or sidewalk, injures herself, and cannot get back on her feet? Am I not allowed to render assistance?" The answer was an emphatic "no." If at your doorstep, the Muslim woman offers her hand to you, then it is safe to shake her hand. But let her make the call. Likewise, the host woman should never offer a sisterly side hug to a Muslim man. Maintain these boundaries until you learn through your ongoing interaction where your Muslim friends stand on these issues. It would not be inappropriate to ask what practice they prefer. Doing so with grace and respect will communicate your sensitivity and appreciation of their cultural practices.

In a similar vein, children of opposite gender who have reached puberty should not be sent off to another part of the house to play. Once a child reaches puberty, the gender boundaries kick in. For Muslims, the age of maturity for a girl is nine, and for a boy fourteen. Why nine for girls? That artificially early age is probably due to Muhammad having consummated his marriage to Aisha when she was nine years old. Placing the age of maturity later than nine would imply that Muhammad had sex with his new wife before she reached puberty. Regardless, boys and girls should never be alone with one another once they become of age. It is assumed that something untoward would likely take place.

Along these same lines, and echoing what we mentioned earlier about formality, hosts should err on the side of conservative attire. Women should not wear shorts, tops that are sleeveless or low-cut, or anything tight-fitting. Men should take care to wear looser slacks, and a long-sleeved shirt would be preferable to short-sleeved. Teen-aged children, especially girls, should follow these same rules. Your Muslim guests will, by no means, expect you to wear Islamic outfits. We should avoid wearing anything that draws attention to the shapes of our bodies, or anything that shows much skin.

Entertainment

As with any new friend we want to build the relationship to a deeper level. Television and movies are probably not good options since intimate conversation is very difficult with all eyes on a screen. Many Muslims, especially those that may have arrived in the West more recently, assume that "America is Christian" such that everything on our TVs and in our movies is likewise "Christian."

We will return to this point later in the book, but for now we should remind ourselves that what appears on our television screens, even in prime time and on supposedly "family friendly" stations, can sometimes be quite immoral. I will forego the sermon concerning our own television viewing habits and simply say we do not want any of this to appear on our television screen while we are entertaining our Muslim friends. They might assume our personal moral standards allow for whatever it is we allow on our televisions. If something immoral appears, our standing in their eyes as moral and spiritual people will suffer.

Bibles

Believe it or not, how you treat *your* Bible can be important to a Muslim. In Islam, the Qur'an takes on an iconic status. Even the paper, the cover, and the ink are often seen as holy. There was a time in Islamic history when the raging debate was how to deal with worn out Qur'ans. Throwing them in the trash would be not only irreverent but sinful; an offense to God. Some theologians suggested burying them. Opponents were aghast at the thought that someone might step on the burial site, or worse, that a human or animal might relieve itself on the ground over it. Other theologians suggested washing the ink off of the paper, then burning the pages. Opponents considered this to only postpone the problem because the issue then became how to dispose of this now holy water.

It is important to Muslims how the book itself is treated. A Muslim will not place the Qur'an on the ground nor will they place it in a chair. The Qur'an must never be placed under another book, or displayed in the room at a level below any other book. It is unthinkable for a Muslim to highlight or underline in a Qur'an. Some even go so far as to insist that only Muslim hands can touch a Qur'an, as non-Muslim hands are unclean and will defile it. Menstruating Muslim women should not touch the Qur'an either. I was once severely chastised by a Muslim in a bookstore for taking a Qur'an off the shelf in violation of a clear sign warning that only Muslims should touch them. I asked him how a non-Muslim could ever read it and learn to become a Muslim if the seeker could not touch the Qur'an. He had seemingly never thought of that, as he had no answer.

Imagine the testimony we give to the value we place on God's word if we treat our Bibles with any less respect. Notice I am not suggesting we treat the Bible like an icon, as Muslims do the Qur'an. I am simply suggesting we can hinder the cause of the gospel if we treat God's word as though it is no more valuable than the latest paperback novel. I advise placing our study Bibles in our bedrooms, and only displaying them in the common areas of our homes if they are clean, well-bound, and unmarked. Make certain you have not left your morning coffee on the end table on top of your Bible. Make sure no other book in the room is displayed at a higher level than the Bible. If you have bookcases in your home this might create a challenge. Eastern homes often have no books, other than the Qur'an, making this issue irrelevant.

The Bottoms of Your Shoes

In some Muslim cultures, showing anyone the bottoms of your shoes is an insult. For some, even crossing your legs is offensive. Until you learn more about your Muslim friend, don't cross your legs. If you learn that leg crossing is not offensive to your friends, then do so in such a way that the bottom of your shoe does not point toward them.

Prayers at Meals

When it comes time to give thanks for our meal, I suggest we use the opportunity to minister to our Muslim guests. Do not say a perfunctory prayer that only gives lip service to God. Rather, thank God sincerely for

His provision. Then pray God's blessings upon your guests, their children, success in their business or trade and protection from harm. Thank God for bringing them into your life as new friends. Pray unapologetically in Jesus' name. Your guests already assume you are Christian because you are American, because you are friendly and hospitable, or for a number of other possible reasons. Do not shrink from an opportunity to affirm your faith. This will also signal to Muslims that you might be more than cultural Christians, but people who take their faith seriously. In that case, they know should they have questions about Christianity, you are the one to ask.

Cards

In many western homes, playing cards is a common pastime. Countless times I remember cleaning off the dinner table, loading the dishes, making a pot of coffee, and bringing out the cards for a game of Spades or Bridge. True, this is a far better way to socialize than watching a movie or television show. But it is not a good idea with some Muslims. Among conservative Muslims, cards are seen as a tool of gambling. To these Muslims, it does not matter whether you are in fact gambling. Possessing the implements that could be used to gamble is prohibited under the *shari'a* doctrine of *sadd al-dhara'i,* which means "blocking the means." This doctrine provides that a thing may be permissible in itself, but if it can lead to a prohibited activity, then that thing itself becomes prohibited.[31] For example, selling grapes is a perfectly legal activity unless one sells them to a wine maker. In that case, selling grapes becomes illegal. Some Muslims see cards in the same way. There is nothing inherently wrong with cards, but their use might lead to gambling, so they become prohibited.

Meals at the Muslim Home

Many of the items we have already discussed will be equally applicable in the Muslim home. But there are a few more cultural notes to keep in mind when visiting your new friends' home for a meal.

---

31   Mohammad Hashim Kamali, *Principles of Islamic Jurisprudence* (Islamic Texts Society) p.397

Gifts

It is customary to take a small gift to your host when you arrive for a meal. They will have gone to a lot of trouble on your behalf, and it is only polite to acknowledge that by offering a token gift to them upon arrival. The most common gift would be some food item such as fresh fruit, nuts, or pastries. Do not take flowers. Flowers are inappropriate as a gift in many cultures, and in some places, the color of the flower communicates a particular meaning. The gift need not be expensive or elaborate. Something fresh from a deli or produce aisle is better than something manufactured and heavily packaged.

Shoes

Have you ever thought about why we in the West eat on tables? Why our furniture has feet? Why we put our mattresses and box springs on bed frames? Do you ever remember your mother telling you to get up and quit eating on the floor? The reason is we consider the floor *dirty*. This has nothing to do with the presence of soil or germs. It is inherently dirty. Therefore, we have no problem wearing shoes into our homes and across carpet. In most Muslim cultures, and in fact throughout most of the East, everyone removes their shoes upon entering a home. Shoes are considered dirty and the floor is considered clean. Traditionally, the average person in the East has eaten on the floor, slept on the floor, and lived life on the floor. Furniture is a relatively recent and western import.

When you arrive at a Muslim's home, before ringing the doorbell, check outside the door to see if shoes are there. If not, wait until the door is open and discretely look inside to see if there are shoes or a shoe rack. If so, you must remove your shoes. Even if the host insists you don't need to remove yours (trying to respect your culture and keep you feeling comfortable), you should still remove them. They will silently appreciate it.

Be a Learner

Don't be the "ugly American" who thinks the best of everything originated in the United States. He thinks we are smarter, better educated, and more enlightened. Noting our relative standard of living and the incredible generosity of Americans, who aid the needy the world over, the "ugly American" develops an attitude of superiority. He is happy to help the less fortunate, often even sacrificially, but does so from a pedestal. The recipient appreciates the help but resents the attitude. Everyone is susceptible to such an attitude and it is poison to relationships. The effective minister to Muslims must double-check his attitude, and renew a Christ-like spirit of humility and servanthood toward all.

When we engage in relationships with Muslims, we must understand that every culture from every nation has things to teach us. There are innumerable ways that any one culture is superior to another, including our own. Those from Muslim-majority countries often put Westerners to shame when it comes to things like hospitality, loyalty, and depth of friendship. Muslim societies are responsible for wonderful advances in mathematics, medicine, astronomy, and other fields. We can learn a lot from our Muslim friends, and we will be richer for it, if we take advantage of the opportunity.

As we develop our relationships with Muslims, we want to express interest in their home countries. We want to ask about music, holidays, foods, handicrafts, languages, important historical events and fine arts. Have fun exchanging information about all areas of life. Learn how to make the foods they enjoy on special occasions. What do they do on holidays? What unique holidays do they celebrate? Do they have a special language they spoke at home as opposed to the national language? What is that language like? The questions are innumerable. Ask about their faith. Do they celebrate Ramadan? Have they found a suitable mosque? Showing a genuine interest in them and in all aspects of their life is one way to demonstrate love and acceptance.

If your Muslim friend offers you a Qur'an, gladly accept it. This is a wonderful ministry opportunity. Read the Qur'an and make note of verses that puzzle you or which say something that sound strange to you. Go back to your friend and ask them about a verse or two. Odds are they will never have heard that verse before. Most Muslims have never read the Qur'an. They are like most cultural Christians. They consider themselves Muslim because they were born to Muslim parents. They might engage in the ritual prayers and ritual fasts, but don't bother to read or study the Qur'an. Further, according to Islamic theology, the Qur'an exists only in the Arabic language in which it was revealed. Translations of the Qur'an are not considered the Qur'an, but only a commentary on the Qur'an. For the non-Arabic speaking Muslim, there is little value in reading the

Qur'an in their own language. The reason for this is the Qur'an is a guide for memorizing and reciting rather than a text to be studied. Islam requires that the recitations be done in Arabic. For non-Arabic speaking Muslims they may not understand the meaning of what they are reciting but only replicating the sounds. When you ask questions from the Qur'an, it will often expose Muslims for the first time to some of the troubling material therein, and may cause doubt to creep into their minds about it.

While living in the Middle East, my family had a close relationship with a particular Muslim family. One member of that family, a young woman in her early twenties, showed an interest in talking about spiritual things. At one point, I noted the verse in the Qur'an stating that a husband can beat his wife. She reacted very defensively, being certain that God's holy book could never say such a horrible thing. Later, she asked her mother about it and her mother confirmed the presence of the verse. She was visibly troubled and increased her inquiries into Christianity.

On another occasion here in the United States, the president of a Muslim Student's Association on a local university campus denied vehemently that the Qur'an allows men to marry pre-pubescent girls. She considered it slander and a lie. When I showed her the verse, she couldn't believe it, and denied that I had interpreted the verse properly. When I showed her the commentaries of recognized authorities, as well as *shari'a* materials on the topic, she was speechless.

We must be careful here. It is seldom a good idea to argue with someone we want to win to faith. It is even worse to "attack" Islam, Muhammad, or the Qur'an in the presence of our Muslim friends. Do not use anything you read in Part One of this book as ammunition to use against Islam or Muhammad. Our friendships will not last long if we do! We will more than likely do more harm than good. The point is simply that most Muslims have not read the Qur'an, and if we ask them honest questions about what we read, it can open the door to spiritual conversations. We can use what we read in the Qur'an as a springboard to move the discussion to the New Testament and the gospel.

What if our Muslim friend asks us to attend a Friday service at the mosque with them? By all means, go! When I attend mosque at the invitation of a friend I sit next to him but do not engage in any of the body motions of the ritual prayer. I am there to observe and learn, but in no way do I want to engage in any ritual or other activity that legitimizes the religion. By attending mosque with my friend, I am showing an acceptance of him as a person and openness to new ideas. It will be difficult to expect him to accept a Bible from me, or an invitation to church, if I have refused his offers and invitations.

Loving a Muslim More Deeply

Muslims who have made faith decisions for Jesus say the love of a Christian was the number one factor that influenced them to do so. Allowing ourselves to be conduits of God's love to others is one of the most effective evangelistic activities in which we can engage. This presents particular challenges to those of us who have grown up in the West. A real life example will help illustrate this.

I was visiting an Iranian friend in a business district of Dubai, UAE. He managed a store that sold housewares. When I arrived, he served me hot tea as was the custom. Shortly thereafter, another young man came into the store. He was a salesman for one of the store's suppliers. As we all sat drinking tea, I noticed this salesman had not yet begun to talk to my friend about supplies he might need to order. I knew from experience that relationships were critical in this part of the world, but wondered about a man on the job visiting a customer. He explained that he always sat and enjoyed tea with his customers, inquiring about their lives, their families, and other matters that might be shared between friends. I asked how many stores he was expected to visit in the course of a day.

"Oh, maybe three or four," he answered.

"In the West, a salesman would work on a quota, be expected to see as many customers as possible each day, and sell as much as he could. If he failed to meet his quota, he might lose his job," I explained.

"I could never live like that," he said.

Western culture is generally individualistic and accomplishment-driven, as opposed to Eastern Culture which is communal and relational. In the West, we value independence, autonomy, self-reliance, and self-determination. Many of the figures that embody our culture, and speak to the ideals we value, are used in advertising. Advertising icons like the Marlboro man and "the most interesting man in the world" appeal to these values. Further, we expect people to make decisions about jobs, education, where to live, and who to marry based on what is in a person's own self-interest.

Eastern culture is often the opposite. A person is not judged on his accomplishments but on the breadth and depth of his relationships. Interconnectedness among groups, such as family and community, is highly valued. People make decisions based on how they impact the immediate family, the extended family, and even the broader community. Individualism and autonomy are seen as undesirable qualities, even signs of weakness and dysfunction. Friendships are close, intimate and loyal.

In the Middle East, a Muslim friend called and asked me what was wrong.

"Nothing's wrong," I said. "Why?"

"Have I done something to offend you or hurt your feelings?"

"No, not at all," I replied. "Why do you ask?"

"Well," he said, "you haven't called me or visited me in a long time."

"We saw each other three or four days ago," I said.

"Yes," he said, "that's true. But in this part of the world real friends don't go more than a day or two without visiting each other, or at least talking on the phone."

"Really? In the United States, I might not see or talk to a friend for several weeks, and think nothing of it."

"Then you're not really friends!"

If we intend to minister the love of God to our Muslim neighbor we will need to make a cultural transformation. Whether a person *experiences* our love is the important thing, not just that we have a feeling of love for them in our hearts. One goal of our lives is to be so transformed into the likeness of Christ that people are *impacted* by His love flowing through us. This is equally true for Muslims. But this requires us to meet them where they are, to enter their cultural and relational world, and impact them with love on their terms. Western relationships are generally superficial. Thus, we will need to become much more relational and much more intimate in our relationships if we hope to minister the love of God to our Muslim friends.

What does this cultural transformation involve? It involves living more *biblically.* You might be surprised to hear that the New Testament embodies a culture. I call it *biblical culture.* Think about one of Paul's metaphors for the Body of Christ. He says we are all one body, such that when any part of the body hurts, the whole body hurts. This illustrates the closeness, the intimacy, and the depth that should characterize our relationships. There are also dozens of verses that either directly or indirectly command us to minister to each others' emotional needs. We are to minister things like comfort, acceptance, approval, encouragement, support, appreciation and many others. Understanding how to minister these things to a particular person requires knowing them intimately. It means knowing what will bless them in these ways given their particular background and life experience. We have to know their hurts, fears, and weaknesses and they have to know ours. Imagine living in a close-knit community where everyone knows each other so well that they know exactly what to say and when to say it. We each receive encouragement, strength, joy, compassion and any number of other blessings from the group, and in the way that is most meaningful to each person.

Unfortunately, most Christians in the West do not obey these relational commands because these verses do not fit our cultural context. Our eyes simply move past these verses with a nod to how true and wonderful they are, but with no idea what it might look like to actually live them out. On many occasions, I have asked audiences whether they have ever "confessed their sins to one another" (James 5:16). I rarely see a raised hand. Confessing our sins to others involves more vulnerability, more intimacy, and more honesty than we are comfortable with in our culture.

We must remember that God does not give us commandments just because He is God and can do whatever He wants. All of God's commandments are rational. They each carry with them the promise of blessings, health and well-being when we obey them, and harm, damage and pain when we fail to obey them. This is easy to see if we consider commandments against murder or adultery. Although the effects are harder to see, the commands to minister to each others' relational needs are no different. God designed us to live abundant and healthy lives because our relational needs are met in the context of a close, intimate community of believers. When these relational needs go unmet, we suffer detriment, pain and deprivation. We see this all around us, even within the Body of Christ. But rather than examining whether we are really living according to all that God commands, we attribute these pathologies to man's fallenness. Irritability, anger outbursts, insecurities, fears, addictive behaviors, "workaholism," loneliness, eating disorders, sleeping disorders, "escaping" into books, movies, sports, or the internet, pornography and issues with spending or hoarding are all sin. But what if we are susceptible to certain of these sins because we have been living apart from the depth and intimacy within the Body of Christ that God intended? If we are really as serious about sin as we say we are, wouldn't we want to explore all possible ways to eradicate it?

In short, if we really want to minister God's love to people we need to learn God's way of doing so. We must look for ways to impact people around us in the area of the "each other" or "one another" commands.

A few years ago, while leading a Bible study among Muslims and former Muslims who had converted to Christ, I read a part of 1 Corinthians 11:2: "I praise you for ..." and announced that we were going to actually "do" this verse in our meeting that night. I asked people to praise, or appreciate, others within the group. Each person was to acknowledge another person for something they had done that was meaningful or for a positive character quality. It started slowly but after a few attempts everyone got involved appreciating others in the group. Upon hearing how they had been a blessing to others or simply being acknowledged for some of their positive qualities the tears began to flow. Months and even years later, various ones among the group mentioned that the Bible "doing" that night was one of the most memorable and meaningful times they had ever spent with other believers.

Here is a breakdown of some of the "one another" verses, together with what it might look like to minister these verses to another person.[32]

Ministering Love to One Another

Acceptance (Romans 15:7) – Ministering acceptance means receiving one another willingly and unconditionally, especially when one's behavior has been less than perfect. It might mean opening our hearts fully to another without regard to their faults, weaknesses, struggles, or sinful behavior. It would mean not allowing another person's faults to create a barrier or hindrance to our "imparting not only the gospel but our very lives" to them.

Affection (Romans 16:16) – This means expressing care and closeness through *appropriate* physical touch and loving words, such as "I love you" or "I care about you".

---

32 For the teaching in this section, including *Ministering Love to One Another*, I am deeply indebted to David and Teresa Ferguson, Lewis and Lacy Alexander and the entire team at Center for Relational Leadership, P.O. Box 201808, Austin, TX 78720; www.greatcommandment.net.

Appreciation (Praise) (1 Corinthians 11:2) – Ministering appreciation might mean expressing personal thanks, praise, or commendation to one another for another's work, effort, accomplishments, or sacrifice. It might mean taking note of and mentioning how meaningful these things have been to us without focusing on where they fell short, could have done better, or mistakes they made.

Approval (Romans 14:18) – Ministering approval might mean acknowledging and expressing gratefulness for another's character qualities. It might mean thinking and speaking well of them. Character qualities we might affirm in another would include: attentiveness, availability, boldness, cautiousness, compassion, contentment, creativity, decisiveness, deference, dependability, determination, diligence, discernment, discretion, endurance, enthusiasm, fairness, faith, flexibility, forgiveness, generosity, gentleness, gratefulness, hospitality, humility, initiative, joyfulness, love, loyalty, meekness, neatness, obedience, patience, persuasiveness, punctuality, resourcefulness, responsibility, reverence, security, self-control, sensitivity, sincerity, thoroughness, thriftiness, tolerance, truthfulness, understanding, virtue, and wisdom.

Attention (Care) (Acts 27:3) – Ministering attention might mean conveying appropriate interest, concern and care for another, taking thought of another, or "entering into another's world." It might mean sacrificing some of our time to express interest in or participate in things that another finds important or interesting. We might minister attention by expressing interest in spending time with another, and allowing them to decide how that time will be spent. A parent might play with a child at whatever game or activity the child chooses. A spouse might dedicate an afternoon or evening to join in whatever hobby or pastime their spouse enjoys. A friend might inquire about progress another is making on a painting, or how their favorite sports team is performing, or whether they have found time to engage in some favorite activity.

Comfort (Empathy) (Romans 12:15) – Ministering comfort means responding to a hurting or disappointed person with words, feelings, and touch; hurting with and for others in the midst of their grief, pain, or disappointment; or to console with tenderness. It might mean that we convey to them that we love them enough that we literally hurt with them when they hurt, or share in their disappointment when they are disappointed. It means much more than saying "I'm sorry".

Encouragement (1 Thessalonians 5:11, Hebrews 10:24) – Ministering encouragement means urging another to persist and persevere toward a goal, and to stimulate one another toward love and good deeds. It might mean expressing confidence in their abilities, reminding them of the worthiness of the goal or deed and the original reasons they undertook the task, and care for the struggle that they might be currently experiencing in persevering.

Respect (Honor) (Romans 12:10) – Ministering respect means valuing and regarding one another highly, and treating one another as important. It means to honor one another. Ministering respect might mean consulting with another over a decision that impacts their life, and discussing the decision with them before making it. It might mean valuing the ideas, opinions, and perspectives of another. It might mean you treat the thoughts or opinions of others as important factors in your decision-making process.

Security (Peace) (2 Thessalonians 3:16) – Ministering security means you ensure harmony in relationships and provide freedom from fear or threat of harm in those relationships. This might mean never threatening or discussing the possibility of breaking off the relationship, whether through divorce or separation in marriage or otherwise. It might mean repeatedly assuring commitment and dedication to the relationship. It might mean reconciling conflict promptly, and communicating that such reconciliation is very important to you.

Support (Galatians 6:2) – Ministering support means coming alongside and gently helping another with a problem or struggle by providing appropriate assistance. It might mean looking for ways to lighten another's burden without regard for your own workload or whose "job" it is to do the task.

A part of what it means to truly love another person as God desires is to look for opportunities to minister these verses to them. Most often, this will mean getting to know them at a deeper level than that with which we are comfortable, and letting them get to know us in the same way. But sometimes we can discern what people might need based upon their general life circumstances.

Imagine seeing a woman in a grocery store, dressed completely in black robes, and several young children at her feet. We might suspect she is Muslim. We might suspect that since most Americans treat Muslims with indifference at best, and hostility at worst, this woman feels lonely and isolated. Perhaps, she is hurt by the treatment she has received in her new country. She may dread trips out in public for fear of the stares, glances, or worse that she might experience. She is likely living apart from her extended family that would support her if she were still "back home." She may not even have other Muslim friends. Her husband may or may not be helpful with any of her household pressures and duties. In what way do you imagine a female follower of Jesus might be able to impact this Muslim woman's heart in a powerful way? Can you imagine how this lonely, hurting woman might feel if someone looked at her, smiled, and said "salaam?" What if she went on to introduce herself, expressing through her eyes, tone of voice, and body language an attitude of warmth and acceptance? Inquiries about children and family might lead to invitations to tea, children's play dates, or baby-sitting for each other. A warm, loving relationship might develop in which spiritual conversations take place and this Muslim woman comes to meet the God who is the author of the love she experiences through her new Christian friend.

Next, imagine a young man named Muhammad working behind the counter at a local convenience store. Muhammad has an engineering degree from a prestigious university in his home country. He came to the United States hoping to secure a good job and a stable life for his family, planning to send for them in a few short years. Instead, he has faced discrimination because of his name and his religion and has not found a decent job. He ultimately took whatever job he could find. He is desperately lonely and ashamed that he has not been able to provide for his family. What's more, customers treat him as clearly inferior, if they acknowledge his existence at all. Occasionally, someone will tell him to go back to where he came from, which hurts him more than one could know.

What if a male follower of Jesus took a few moments and looked Muhammad in the eye, said hello, and when the transaction finished, said "God bless you." What if on the next visit to the store, this Christ follower took a moment to inquire where Muhammad is from, expressed a welcoming response, and asked about Muhammad's family? Upon learning that Muhammad lives half a world away from his wife and children, what if we expressed regret over the loneliness Muhammad feels and hurt with him over his separation from his family. Perhaps Muhammad would feel blessed to receive an invitation for a home-cooked meal.

Imagine a Muslim doctor. She sees patients all day, and they are all pleasant enough. But upon returning home, none of her neighbors know her name, nor does she know theirs. There is no community, no mutual caring, and no support. She is financially comfortable, but relationally and emotionally, she is withering and dry. How might she feel if her neighbors, a family of Christ followers, see her in her front yard on their nightly walk, stop and inquire about her and invite her over for tea?

We can build relationships with Muslims by exhibiting a Christ-like love to them. As these relationships deepen through ministry to heart-felt needs and as we are vulnerable about our own struggles and weaknesses, we can enter into deeper relationships. Relationships like this are a far more fruitful context for sharing the gospel than our traditional, "drive-by" evangelism methods.

CHAPTER 6

Sharing the Gospel with Muslims

Initial Matters

SHORTLY AFTER BECOMING A Christian at the age of eighteen, I was introduced to the concept of evangelism. I remember one particular Sunday School teacher that began each lesson by asking us to tell about our witnessing activities the prior week. For those who had not shared their faith during the past week, he said their week had been wasted.

It was within this environment that I learned evangelism tools such as Evangelism Explosion, Continuing Witness Training, the "Roman Road," and the use of small tracts to communicate the gospel. I learned to share my testimony, highlighting my life prior to Christ, how I came to know Christ, and how my life changed thereafter, all within 90 seconds or less. The subtle message of all of this training was that the important thing was to "get the gospel out there." Whether people accepted the gospel was somehow secondary. I have come to call this philosophy "drive-by" evangelism or "hit and run" evangelism. The results of these methods were meager. With Muslims, one might even say these methods are counter-productive.

Islam provides that if a Muslim changes his religion, he should be killed. Muslims view conversion to Christianity or any other religion to be among the worst sins possible. Many Muslims will shut down any relationship at the first hint that the Christian has designs on converting them. This is why we must focus on loving them into the kingdom. This is also why traditional methods of evangelism are likely to be counter-productive with Muslims. This is not as big a hurdle as it may seem at first.

The Holy Spirit is always the one who does the converting. 1 Corinthians 4:3 says: "And even if our gospel is veiled, it is veiled to those who are perishing, in whose case the god of this world has blinded the minds of the unbelieving, that they might not see the light of the gospel of the glory of Christ, who is the image of God." Satan has blinded the minds of all unbelievers so they cannot see the truth. No amount of our effort, cleverness in sharing, or persuasive ability will result in a Muslim coming to faith in Christ. The Holy Spirit must remove the spiritual blindness before Muslims can see the truth.

Our role in the conversion process is simply to educate our Muslim friend on that truth. This can be done in an educational way. Don't convert anyone; don't even try. What I do is educate my Muslim friend on the truths of Christianity. This can be done simply for their edification, so that they might better understand Christianity, or for the sake of having the information. What they do with the truth is between them and God.

This tack has many advantages. First, the Muslim does not think you have been "playing" at friendship in order to witness to them. Second, there is no effort to convert them, thus avoiding the negative reaction that often accompanies such efforts. Third, it will motivate me to pray more fervently, since only a movement by the Holy Spirit will result in the desired outcome.

We must also remember to remain patient when beginning a ministry to Muslims. It is a far more monumental thing for a Muslim to convert to Christianity than it is for a Westerner to change religions. A Muslim follower of Jesus will most often be rejected by his or her family, ostracized by the community, and be thought a traitor to their country, race, and heritage. They can sometimes be killed. A Christian must be sensitive to these considerations and understand the possible consequences.

I remember hearing about a survey of Turkish believers. They were asked how much time passed between the time they came to believe the truth of the gospel and the time they made a faith decision for Jesus. The average response was eighteen months. This was not how long it took them to accept the truth of the gospel, but how long after they believed did they finally trust Christ.

Ministry to Muslims is a long-term proposition. We might invest years before seeing fruit. It is helpful to keep in mind that there is kingdom value in simply ministering the whole character of God to another person. We invest in relationships and minister love, compassion, acceptance, respect, approval, support and comfort because that is who God is. This ministry has value in itself. Our desire is to love Muslims into the kingdom, no matter how long it takes, and even knowing that they may never come to faith.

It is important that we never say a critical word about Muhammad, the Qur'an or Islam. Muslims rarely come to faith in Jesus when their own belief system is attacked. Like anyone else, they will become defensive. They will withdraw from constructive dialogue. And they will probably lose respect for you. In short, by attacking Islam we damage our own cause, and likely burn any bridges between ourselves and our Muslim friend.

Finally, remember that prayer is the key to any effective ministry. We need to pray daily for the Holy Spirit to open the hearts of our Muslim friends. Have other Christians, churches, Sunday School classes, Bible studies, or other groups join in praying. We can also add fasting to our prayers. "For our struggle is not against flesh and blood, but against the rulers, against the powers, against the world forces of this darkness, against the spiritual forces of wickedness in the heavenly places." Ephesians 6:12.

Communicating the Gospel

Given all we've covered so far, how do we share the truth of the gospel in an effective way? First, we want to give our Muslim friend a gift of the New Testament. Here is what I suggest. Give them a New Testament on a normal, gift-giving occasion, like Christmas, Easter or their birthday. Why? Because they are less likely to see this as an attempt to convert them, but see it as a thoughtful gift of something meaningful.

I suggest wrapping the New Testament in very nice paper with a bow like you would in the most formal occasion. This communicates the value of the contents inside. Also, buy the nicest quality, hard cover edition of the New Testament you can find. Remember that Muslims often idolize the Qur'an, and Qur'ans are often very ornate and expensive. To them, books of the greatest value are made with the most honoring and respectful materials possible. A pocket paperback is not worthy of the Word of God. Of course, if a pocket paperback is all you can find, it will be better than nothing.

Pay attention to the language of the New Testament you give your Muslim friend. We want to give God's Word to them in their "heart language," that is, the language with which they are most comfortable. They might be fluent in English but be more comfortable in the language they spoke growing up. For them, speaking English might involve focus and concentration. Their heart language flows easily and effortlessly. They dream in their heart language. They read poetry in their heart language. They experience emotion in their heart language. When reading the New Testament, we do not want them focusing intellectually on the meaning of the words. Rather, we want the words to minister to the innermost places of their heart, to evoke emotion, to touch them.

Determining your friend's heart language is not difficult. You can ask them in which language they are most comfortable. You can ask them whether they have forgotten much of their home language. Keep in mind that after several years of non-use, people lose ability in any language, including their heart language. You can ask in what language they would prefer to read a book. And, you can be fairly sure that if your Muslim friend was born in an English-speaking country, or has lived in such a country for decades, an English language New Testament will be fine. If they have recently arrived from their home country within the last year or two, their heart language will usually be the language of home.

Notice I suggested giving them a New Testament rather than the whole Bible. The reason for this is the Muslim will likely know almost nothing about the Bible, and will start reading at Genesis 1:1. If they do, they will give up before finishing Leviticus. Rather, we want them to start at Matthew 1:1 and encounter the person of Jesus immediately.

Where do you find New Testaments in foreign languages? If you have internet, first try an online bookstore. Try the American Bible Society or International Bible Society. There are many ministry organizations dedicated to reaching people groups speaking almost every language on earth. With a little internet research, you will be able to identify ministries to the people group to which your Muslim friend belongs. These ministries will be able to provide you with New Testaments and other resources in the desired language.

At other gift-giving occasions, we can give our Muslim friends additional items. One such gift might be the "Jesus" film. Another film is "God's Story" which is available for order online. The variety and quality of resources available in most languages increase yearly. Contact one of the ministry organizations dedicated to your friend's people group for advice on appropriate resources.

With each of these gifts, we hope to prompt spiritual conversations, answering whatever questions they have about whatever it is they read or watch. As they ask questions, don't think you have to have all the answers. Feel free to admit you don't know the answer to their question, but will find the answer. You may be able to search and find the answer together. You may need to consult commentaries, ask questions of other Christians, or ask your pastor for help. The point is to help them understand and seriously consider what they are reading. In the course of answering their questions, we want to cover all the essentials of the gospel and address theological issues Muslims might have with Christian truths. We will consider this in the next chapter.

If your friend does not ask any questions within a few weeks after receiving your gift, then it is fine to ask them if they have had a chance to read anything from the New Testament, or watch the video, as the case may be. Don't press it if they haven't, but offer to answer any questions they might have upon reading or watching. Make sure you and your circle of Christian friends are praying fervently for them.

Keep in mind two things. We don't need to launch into long theological monologues, trying to cover everything in one or two conversations. All of this will be new to the Muslim, and small doses of truth spread out over time will more likely sink in. Also, we do not have to wait for the Muslim to initiate spiritual conversations. We can casually share biblical truth whenever the occasion warrants it. Feel free to quote a Bible verse applicable to whatever life situation arises. We can also offer to pray for our friend about any issues or problems they are facing. Pray together with your Muslim friend over issues of concern in their life, as well as issues of concern in your own life. Being sensitive, compassionate and respectful, while not forcing the issue, will likely be well-received and effective.

It is important to remember we must not make "ministry" a one-way street. Remember to avoid the "ugly American" syndrome. In Christian ministry, this manifests itself in a sense of superiority over those to whom we desire to minister. We may unwittingly think we know the truth and have all the answers, and thus our Muslim friends have nothing to offer us. This is arrogant, unbiblical, and poison to any meaningful relationship. Yes, Christianity is true and Islam is false. But Christians are not inherently better than Muslims or anyone else. Muslims have much to offer us, and we can learn much from them. Every culture and society on earth excels at some trait or characteristic, and we can learn from all of them. We do not have a monopoly on wisdom, knowledge or experience, and can benefit from a ministry of these things to us by our Muslim friends.

Any meaningful relationship involves mutual giving, honor and respect. We must treat Muslims as equals and not simply recipients of our ministry. As we relate to our Muslim friends, we need to allow them to care for us, pray for us, and invest in our lives. We need to be vulnerable about our own struggles and fears, our own weaknesses and challenges. As we do so, we likewise reveal to our friends how we deal with these problems, how we pray, and how we trust Jesus to help us. Then, when Jesus intervenes in our lives, helps us and heals us, this provides a powerful testimony of the power of Jesus, and the way we walk with him, talk with him, and trust him with all aspects of our lives. This is a far more powerful testimony than simply a ministry of preaching theological truths and is far more likely to minister to the heart of the Muslim.

Although everyone is different, a certain pattern often emerges. Many times I have had Muslims read the New Testament and say things like: "I am still a Muslim, but I really love Jesus." This is an important milestone along the way. Often times, the Muslim will compare what they know of Muhammad with what they are reading of Jesus. As we said previously, we do not need to point out the contrasts. They will do that themselves and be impressed with Jesus. When we reach this point, we will want to slowly and diplomatically begin to emphasize the "hard" claims of Jesus. These include his identity, the nature and attributes of God, the sinful nature of humanity, and the consequences of these truths for us. The Muslim must come to understand that he or she is a sinner who cannot save themselves through their own efforts or obedience to religious rituals. They are hopeless without the sacrificial death of Jesus. It is often at this stage that the Muslim's preconceived theological objections take on greater importance. The next chapter will be important in this respect.

The Christian witness will also remember the folk beliefs of many Muslims, discussed previously. In many contexts, the Muslim's spiritual life is oriented around superstitious practices designed to obtain protection from evil forces, curses and spells. On the other hand, the Muslim will engage in similar practices to obtain blessings and benefit from positive spiritual forces. In this context, the Christian should emphasize the power

Jesus has over all of these forces, and that He is the source of every spiritual blessing. One might read and discuss New Testament accounts illustrating the power of Jesus over demonic forces, and passages teaching that Jesus is the creator of everything in heaven and on earth, visible and invisible. See, for example, Colossians 1:16-17. The Christian should pray fervently and fast for the Muslim for whom these superstitions are important. We must remember we are engaged in spiritual warfare.

CHAPTER 7
Dealing with Theological Objections

ISLAM ARRIVED ON THE scene six hundred years after Christianity. Muhammad and the early Muslims knew a few things about Christianity due to exposure to the Ebionites, a heretical sect in the area of western Arabia. Much of what the Qur'an says about Christianity is wrong, but Muslims view the Qur'an as the inerrant, perfectly preserved revelation of God. To them, it is inconceivable the Qur'an could err in any way. These mistaken beliefs Muslims have about Christianity constitute significant barriers between the Muslim and faith in Christ.

In most cases, your Muslim friend will not confront you with these beliefs. They do not want to offend you by stating they think something you believe is wrong. In the course of your friendship, as you weave in and out of spiritual conversations over time, it will be important to look for opportunities to address these issues. You will want to clear up these misunderstandings in a brief conversational way, rather than handing them a book on the topic. Below we will list the most common theological barriers and an effective way to address them.

Reliability of the New Testament

According to Islam, all the prophets throughout history, and all the holy books they brought, taught Islam. The reason we don't see Islam in their teachings is because over time humans have corrupted the messages of these prophets and altered their books. Muslims recognize Jesus as one of the five greatest prophets in history. But like all other prophets, Muslims believe Jesus' original message was Islam, and the New Testament taught Islam. Islam also teaches that the New Testament prophesied the coming of Muhammad. They claim that, over the years, the church changed and corrupted the New Testament so that neither Islam nor Muhammad appear anywhere in its pages today. Thus, for Muslims, the New Testament is unreliable. Given this belief, many of them will instantly reject any verse of the Bible or teaching of Christianity that does not agree with Islamic doctrine. It will be hard for a Muslim to trust his eternal security to Jesus if he cannot trust the truth of scripture's teaching.

In addressing this issue, we need a short, accurate and convincing description of how we got the New Testament, why we know it has not been corrupted or changed, and why we know it is trustworthy. Providing a book on the topic will not likely be helpful. Rather, we need an explanation that takes only a minute or two. By necessity, such an explanation will have to greatly summarize a lot of material, smooth over a few rough edges, and leave out a lot of information. One possible explanation is the following.

The original manuscripts of the New Testament books were written on parchment, which the people knew would deteriorate rather quickly. Like all other important documents of the period, professional experts made copies of the documents in order to preserve the text on newer materials as the older ones wore out. These professionals were extremely careful to copy everything perfectly.

As the church grew and expanded, each local group of believers wanted its own set of copies of the twenty-seven separate books of the New Testament. These scribes eventually made thousands of copies of the New Testament books which were spread all over the Middle East, North Africa, and in parts of Europe and Central Asia.

If someone wanted to change the text of any of these books, this is what they would need to do. First, identify the location of every copy of every book in hundreds of locations where all the copies were kept. To be successful, they could not miss any copies. They would then need to break in and steal all the copies without ever getting caught. Next, they would need to forge changes so expertly that no one would notice. The changes would need to be exactly the same in every copy of each book. They would then need to break in again and replace the copies without being caught. Finally, the changes must be such that the Christians would never notice the words they knew so well, and in many cases had memorized, read differently than before. This story is so ridiculous that no thinking person can believe it happened.

Further, if it did happen, why didn't the Qur'an say so? Why didn't Muhammad say so? Instead, the Qur'an speaks very highly of the Christian scriptures, and tells Christians to believe in and follow what their scriptures say. How could the Qur'an say this if the New Testament had been corrupted? It makes no sense to say the New Testament was corrupted after Muhammad's time, since thousands of manuscript copies date hundreds of years before Muhammad, and our Bibles are translated from those ancient manuscripts. In short, the claim that the New Testament has been corrupted from its original form is a myth.

The importance of this issue cannot be overstated. Some years ago, a team of Lebanese Christians ventured north to a European capital where many Gulf Arabs vacation during the summer. Over the course of two weeks, this team of Christians led twenty-nine Muslims from Kuwait, Bahrain, Qatar, the UAE and Saudi Arabia to saving faith in Jesus. In describing their methods they emphasized prioritizing this issue. In their initial discussions with the Muslims, they provided an explanation on the reliability of the New Testament similar to the one described above. They reported that once they addressed the issue in this way the Muslims came to faith readily.

The explanation provided above should be persuasive, and lend authority to scripture in the eyes of the Muslim. However, if we encounter a Muslim for whom this is a particularly important issue, and we discern that it may be a pivotal stumbling block, we can refer them to some of the various books that delve into the matter in more detail. Ask your pastor or Bible study leader for recommendations.

Son of God

The Qur'an purports to correct the Christian belief that Jesus is the Son of God. However, the Qur'an says Christians believe Son of God means "offspring." In other words, Muslims think affirming Jesus to be the Son of God means Christians believe God had intimate relations with Mary, and Jesus is their child. If true, this would be blasphemous to the Muslim and the Christian as well. This is not what the Bible teaches and not what Christians believe. It will be very important to help Muslims understand what the Bible really teaches about the phrase "Son of God."

The most important thing to remember is the phrase "Son of God" is a title, not a description. Luke 1:32 says "He shall be great and *shall be called* the Son of the Most High; ..." Romans 1:4 says Jesus "*was declared* the Son of God with power ..." Thus, the phrase has nothing to do with any relationship between God and Mary. However, it will not be enough to state what it does not mean. So, what does it mean?

Some years back I was in my Arab landlord's office. I was visiting him to make my annual rent payment. He sat behind his desk as we enjoyed Arabic coffee, made from raw coffee beans and cardamom, and chatted about family and life in general. At one point, he asked me how Christians could believe God came down to earth and had sex with Mary. I assured him we did not believe this. Apparently because he knew the Qur'an, he insisted we do believe it. My denials had no impact on him. From this encounter I learned it would not be enough to deny a false understanding. I needed to give him the truth to replace his belief.

In the Old Testament, the phrase "Son of God" carries one of three meanings. It could refer to an angel, to a pious individual Israelite, or to the nation of Israel as a whole. Between the testaments, as evidenced by the Dead Sea Scrolls, the phrase "Son of God" took on a different meaning. In the decades before Jesus was born, the phrase came to refer to the coming Messiah. So when Jesus was called *the* Son of God, Jews understood this to mean Jesus was the Messiah. But in New Testament usage, the title went further. The Jews understood Jesus to be saying he was divine (John 5:18. See also Hebrews 1:8).

The phrase also carries cultural implications that further indicate divinity. First century Palestine was strongly paternalistic. Sons were highly valued as the means by which the family name was preserved. Sons inherited the family estate and the family reputation. A man's sons were his agents in public, able to bind him to contracts and incur debts on his behalf. In a very real sense, a man's sons represented the man himself. Dealing with a son was like dealing with the father in person. The son was the embodiment of the father. This was especially true when a man had only one son. Taking the theological and cultural implications together, "Son of God" was a clear assertion of divinity.

While the true biblical meaning rules out the Muslim misunderstanding of the phrase "Son of God," it also brings us face to face with another theological objection – the Trinity.

The Trinity

The Qur'an mistakenly corrects Christians for believing Jesus was the offspring of God. The Qur'an also mistakenly corrects Christians for believing in three gods. Polytheism, or associating partners with God, is the gravest of sins in Islam. In the course of our spiritual conversations with Muslims, it will be important to dispel the idea that belief in the Trinity is belief in three gods. We need to emphasize that Christians believe in only one God in three persons.

The Trinity is a difficult doctrine. Our goal is not to lead the Muslim to a complete understanding of the Trinity since no one grasps it fully. We simply want to remove a mistaken understanding of the Trinity as a barrier between the Muslim and saving faith in Jesus. While none of the illustrations commonly used for the Trinity are complete or totally accurate theologically, they can be useful in achieving our task.

The illustration I like best is that of water. I can put a pot of water on a stove, dip some out of the pot and put it in a freezer. After a while, the water in the freezer will solidify, and some of the water in the pot will turn to steam. Thus, from the one pot of water we will have liquid, solid, and gas. I can then return the ice to the pot, where it turns back to liquid, and capture the steam, where it will do the same. Like water, which is one substance in three forms, the Trinity is one God in three persons.

I am aware of one case in which a Muslim has come to faith in Jesus while admitting he did not understand the Trinity. He trusted God could make it clear to him if God wished, or he would simply accept the doctrine without understanding it fully.

Sin

A student in a Business Ethics class at a Middle Eastern university stood up to scold his fellow students on their attitude toward sin. "If you were really honest with yourselves, you'd admit you sin at least once per week!" I remember thinking I probably sin once per minute. This incident illustrates the different perspective Muslims have regarding sin. For the Muslim, sins are the "big ones" like murder, rape, adultery, theft, drunkenness and the like. I have had a number of Muslims tell me they have never sinned, thinking they have never committed any of these "big" sins. That conclusion might make sense if we only count the "big ones," and if we consider only affirmative acts as "big ones."

Upon reflection, Muslims will also admit there are smaller sins, but believe God forgives these smaller sins when we are obedient to the Islamic worship rituals of prayer, fasting, and the hajj. Thus, as long as they avoid the big sins and are faithful to the rituals, sin is not a problem for them. What is important to Muslims is maintaining ritual purity. This ceremonial cleanliness is mandatory if the ritual performances are to earn them spiritual merit.

Accordingly, the Christian witness should address the biblical concept of sin. It is important to highlight what the Bible teaches regarding sin in our thought lives. That includes all sorts of ungodly attitudes like pride, selfishness, animosity, ungratefulness, lust, anger, and greed. We can also bring attention to the sins we commit with our words, as well as with words we should say but don't. The point is to have the Muslim consider all the ways in which we sin internally, and all the ways we sin by omission, in addition to our outward sins of commission. It is important for Muslims to come to the realization of the scope and severity of sin. An accurate understanding of sin renders hopeless the notion that we can earn salvation through good works.

In the West, we tend to view sin through the lens of our guilt and innocence. This perspective highlights God's commandments, our violation and guilt, God's judgment and condemnation, and ultimately God's forgiveness. But this understanding doesn't fit as well for those with a different perspective. People from the East often do not share our guilt and innocence worldview. They typically view the world through the lenses of cleanliness and defilement. We see this very clearly in Islam, where ceremonial defilement and ritual washings are important to pious living and spiritual reward. What is often unnoticed by Western Christians is that such a worldview is clearly present in the New Testament. It was important to the Jewish theology Jesus encountered in his interactions with people in first century Palestine.

Jesus teaches that what a person ingests does not defile him, for it goes into the stomach and is passed out the body. That which proceeds out of the heart of a person defiles him. We might ask our Muslim friend how external, ceremonial washings can cleanse internal sins, sins of the heart, sins of attitude and thought, and sins of omission. These sins defile our souls. When our bodies die and only our souls remain, how will defiled souls enter the holy presence of God? If we cannot enter a mosque on earth in a defiled state, how will we enter heaven? If we cannot offer prayers to God in a defiled state, how will God accept our defiled souls into His holy, pure, undefiled heavenly presence?

Implicit in this line of reasoning is an understanding of the attributes of God, including his absolute holiness. Islam teaches that God's attributes are unknowable. We turn next to a discussion of these attributes.

The Attributes of God

Islam teaches that God is too distant for us to comprehend. It teaches that our finite minds can never contemplate or understand any inherent attribute in God. Islam says that humans can only know God by what He does. Thus, it would not make sense to think about God in terms of absolute attributes. However, Muslims and others who have not studied Islamic theology understand instinctively that God is the greatest of all possible beings. He must have certain characteristics, and these characteristics must be absolute. With a little effort, we can help clarify these concepts in the mind of our Muslim friend.

The Bible teaches that God is absolutely just, holy, loving and merciful. All of God's attributes are absolute, and exist and operate to their fullest extent at all times. It is God's absolute justice that mandates all sin must be punished. If any sin is not punished, then God is not *absolutely* just. When we sin, in addition to being guilty and condemned to punishment, we are defiled. This defilement violates God's holiness. Since God's holiness is absolute, this means any sin defiles us and forever separates us from His holy presence. Despite the certainty of our eternal punishment, God's absolute love and mercy are also fully operational. These attributes mean that God would make a way to reconcile us to Himself. On the cross, Jesus took upon himself the punishment we deserved, and his shed blood served to cleanse sin's defilement of our souls. It is only through Jesus' death on the cross that God's justice was satisfied. It is only through Jesus' shed blood that our defilement was cleansed. Through faith in Jesus' accomplished work on the cross, we can now enter God's holy presence and spend eternity there.

The truth of the Christian gospel, and the necessity of Christ's death on the cross proceeds logically from an understanding of God's attributes. We do well to spend time with our Muslim friend in discussion of these attributes. Yet we are faced with another barrier hindering the Muslim's acceptance of these truths – the crucifixion of Jesus.

The Crucifixion

The Qur'an states clearly that Jesus was not crucified, but God made it appear that he was. Rather, he was taken straight to heaven at some time prior to the crucifixion. His facial appearance was placed on an imposter, and the imposter was crucified instead, creating the appearance that it was Jesus on the cross. There is disagreement on the identity of the imposter, but most believe it was Judas. Many Muslims will add that as one of God's greatest prophets, it is inconceivable that the enemies of Jesus could overcome him. God's prophets are always victorious over their enemies. However, Christians know that Jesus submitted his life willingly. While a Muslim may smile and nod respectfully when a Christian talks of the crucifixion, in reality they reject the idea altogether.

It will be hard for a Muslim to repent of his sins and accept the sacrificial death of Jesus on the cross if the Muslim rejects the crucifixion. We will need to address this issue in a persuasive way. There are a vast number of problems with the Qur'an's teaching regarding the crucifixion. We will look at a few of them.

First, if Jesus was taken straight to heaven, it is almost certain his disciples would have seen it or known of it. They spent nearly every moment with Jesus for two years. If God took Jesus to heaven during a moment when he was beyond eyesight of his disciples, they would have at least noticed that Jesus had disappeared.

Second, if Jesus' appearance was placed upon Judas, and it was Judas taken before the authorities, we know how Judas would have responded. He would have protested with all his strength that he was not Jesus, that the authorities had the wrong guy. He would have denied all the claims of Jesus that the authorities found offensive. He would have said whatever they wanted him to say to avoid the beatings, torture and crucifixion. Yet, this traitor Judas spoke and acted *exactly like Jesus would have* in the same circumstances.

Third, the person we saw on the cross acted exactly like we would expect Jesus to act, and the opposite of how we would expect Judas, or another imposter, to act. The person on the cross promised the thief hanging next to him that he would join Jesus in paradise. How could Judas have said that? The person on the cross looked down on his tormentors and asked the Father to forgive them. Would a criminal like Judas have had such selfless compassion and concern for those responsible for his unjust torture? Finally, the person on the cross looked down at Mary and John, and asked John to care for Mary. Only Jesus would be concerned for who would look after His surviving mother. It makes no sense that an imposter would do this.

Fourth, Muslim theologians tell us the facial likeness of Jesus was put on the imposter. If we assume this is true, we can imagine the disciples and others looking upon the person on the cross and seeing Jesus' face. What about the rest of his body? Wouldn't the disciples, who had lived with Jesus daily for two years, have noticed the differences between the body of Jesus and the body of Judas or some other imposter? Would not his mother Mary have noticed such differences?

Fifth, it is difficult to imagine what righteous and holy cause could have prompted God to perpetrate this fraud on His followers. If God really did perpetrate this fraud, what does that say about the character of God? Is a perfectly holy and righteous God really capable of such deception?

Sixth, if God is capable of such deception toward His faithful believers of the time, then could He not also deceive those who follow Islam? If God is capable of such action, with regard to the crucifixion, then He is capable of creating the entire religion of Islam as a similar deception for Muslims. Although this is unthinkable for Muslims, it is the logical conclusion one is compelled to draw if the Qur'anic account of the crucifixion is correct.

Prophecies of Muhammad

The Qur'an states on several occasions that prior scriptures, including the Old and New Testaments, prophesy the coming of Muhammad. Very few Muslims have read either one but assume, since the Qur'an could never be mistaken, that the claim must be true. Since the claim is false, Muslim scholars have gone to great lengths to "find" prophecies of Muhammad in the Bible. Most of the instances they "find" are without merit, but two deserve some attention.

In Deuteronomy 18:15-19, Moses says the following:

> The Lord your God will raise up for you a prophet like me from among you, from your countrymen (also translated "brothers" here and throughout the passage), you shall listen to him. This is according to all that you asked of the Lord your God in Horeb on the day of the assembly, saying, 'Let me not hear again the voice of the Lord my God, let me not see this great fire anymore, or I will die.' The Lord said to me, 'They have spoken well. I will raise up a prophet from among their countrymen like you, and I will put My words in his mouth, and he shall speak to them all that I command him. It shall come about that whoever will not listen to My words which he shall speak in My name, I Myself will require it of him. (New American Standard Version)

Muslim scholars contend the prophet "from among you" through whom God would speak, refers to Muhammad. The most common arguments in favor of this interpretation are as follows. Both Moses and Muhammad were lawgivers, prophets and led military actions. Also, the future prophet would come from the brothers of the Israelites, which must be the Ishmaelites, and Islam teaches that Ishmael was the ancestor of Muhammad.

However, the context shows clearly that Muhammad was not in view. The Jews no longer wanted to hear the voice of God directly, and asked God to provide a mediator. God said He would raise up such a mediator for the Jews, who would deliver His words to them. Jesus fits this description perfectly while the claim for Muhammad is weak. The group from which the prophet would be raised, "your brothers" or "your countrymen," refers to the Jews themselves, not the Ishmaelites. Reference here the number of Old Testament passages that use the phrase "your brothers" to refer to the Israelites. Muhammad was not raised up from among the Jews, but from among the Arabs. Further, the passage claims the prophet would be "like" Moses. While there are a few surface similarities between Moses and Muhammad, there are far more dissimilarities. The parallels between Moses and Jesus clearly align.

Moses and Jesus were both threatened as infants, and both performed signs and wonders. Moses served forty years of preparation in the wilderness, while Jesus served forty days. Both delivered Israel from bondage – Moses from physical bondage in Egypt and Jesus from spiritual bondage from sin. Both spoke with God face to face. Both prophesied future events which prophecies were fulfilled. The Jews rebelled against both. The list could go on.

The other most commonly cited passages are those in John chapters 14 and 15 where Jesus tells of the coming of the Holy Spirit. The Qur'an says at *sura* 61, verse 6 that Jesus promised the coming of a messenger whose name would be Ahmad. Ahmad is an alternate form of the name Muhammad, and means "praised one." In Greek, "praised one" would be *periklytos*. The Greek word in John quotes Jesus as promising the *periclete*, or "Comforter." Muslims contend Christians corrupted the text and changed the word to hide this prophecy of Muhammad.

In response, we would say there is no manuscript evidence for *periklytos*. Every manuscript of John uses *periclete,* and these manuscripts all predate Muhammad by centuries. How would Christians have known about Muhammad and changed these manuscripts centuries before Muhammad appeared on the scene? Thus, there is no evidence whatsoever for the Muslim argument. Secondly, in John 14:17 Jesus, speaking to his disciples, says the *periclete* will be "with you" and "in you." Obviously, Muhammad was never with Jesus' disciples, and certainly never "in them."

Keeping in mind our goal is not to argue or debate, nor to score points, the best response to the allegation that the Deuteronomy passage refers to Muhammad is to say the Bible never mentions Muhammad, and the passage refers to Jesus being raised up from among the Jews. Likewise, with regard to the John passages, we should simply say these are references to the coming of the Holy Spirit, who would indwell the believer. If it appears the matter is a key barrier between the Muslim and faith in Jesus, the Christian should access further material on the topic. See many excellent articles on this and other issues at www.answering-islam.org.

The Gospel of Barnabas

Some Christians are aware that a few "gospels" were written in the second and third centuries in accordance with Gnostic and other heretical theologies. What most Christians are unaware of is that Muslims have their own version of the gospel, entitled *The Gospel of Barnabas*. This so-called gospel tells the story of the life of Jesus from the Muslim perspective and is one of the best-selling books in the Muslim world. Muslims will sometimes say *The Gospel of Barnabas* was written contemporaneously with the four canonical gospels, but survived uncorrupted, and is thus an accurate portrayal of Jesus and his teachings.

There are clear indications that *The Gospel of Barnabas* was not written in the first century, but many centuries later. For instance, *The Gospel of Barnabas* portrays the people storing wine in wooden casks rather than in wineskins made from animal hides, as was the practice in the first century and in many centuries thereafter. The storage of wine in wooden casks did not begin until the Middle Ages in Europe. Further, *The Gospel of Barnabas* references celebrating the year of Jubilee every 100 years, while the biblical cycle is every 49 or 50 years. In the year 1343, Pope Boniface declared the year of Jubilee to fall every 100 years rather than every 50, as it had been up until that time. Thus, *The Gospel of Barnabas* must have been written sometime after the year 1343. *The Gospel of Barnabas* also uses the Latin Vulgate translation of the New Testament, which did not exist until the fourth century.

The earliest manuscript of the book is in Italian and dates to the seventeenth century. While Muslim scholars are well aware of the book today, and refer to it widely, they never mentioned it before the seventeenth or eighteenth century. No Christian writer refers to it before then either. Certainly, someone somewhere would have mentioned it or quoted from it prior to the seventeenth century if it was indeed a first-century document. The fact that the first mention of the book occurs at the same time the first manuscript appears proves it is a seventeenth century document. This, combined with the clear act of attributing events to a period in which they do not belong, prove beyond doubt that *The Gospel of Barnabas* is a late forgery.

Western Culture and Christianity

While in the Middle East, a close friend mine related a poignant story. The friend is an Iranian Christian, and told of a conversation he had with a young man from Saudi Arabia.

"I know all about Christianity," said the young Saudi.

Astonished, the Iranian asked how that was possible in the repressive environment of Saudi Arabia.

"Easy," the Saudi responded. "I watch a Christian movie every night."

"How is that possible in Saudi Arabia?" the Iranian asked skeptically.

"I have HBO."

Although the Saudi's naiveté is humorous, the story reveals a disturbing reality. While this is less true for Muslims who have lived in the West for some time, for those living outside the West, this reality is obvious. The West is Christian. The West is morally corrupt and decadent. Thus, Christianity is morally corrupt and decadent. Islam vigorously guards against such immorality, and one rarely sees such open displays of sexuality and perversion in the Muslim world as one sees in the West. Thus, Islam is superior to Christianity.

One way to address this misunderstanding would be to point out that immorality is built into Islam. The Qur'an provides for polygamy, wife beating, sexual slavery and child marriage. Shi'ite Islam approves temporary marriage, *siqeh*, which might last no more than an hour. There is rampant sexual immorality and perversion in the Muslim world, but it is hidden behind closed doors and ignored by Muslim media in order to protect the image of Islam in the outside world. For instance, I have never encountered a prostitute in the West, but was propositioned by prostitutes in both Dubai and Tehran.

However, this type of response will likely detract from our objectives. The Christian will want to point out that while Western countries were founded on Christian principles, which account for their freedoms and prosperity, they are largely secular and humanist today. Christians object to all the same social and moral pathologies Muslims find offensive. Jesus teaches us marriage is between one man and one woman for life, that sex outside of marriage is sin, and that alluring dress is sinful. We oppose abortion, homosexual activity, drug use, and prostitution. At this point, one might take the opportunity to further explain the biblical teaching on sin.

The Question of Israel

Muslims, both in the Middle East and in the West, ask me one question far more than any other. "Why does the United States support Israel?" There may be very good geopolitical reasons why the United States supports Israel, but they all miss the point. When Muslims ask this question, they are not thinking of high-minded geopolitical considerations. Rather, they have in mind the plight of the Palestinians.

When the state of Israel was created in 1948, some Christians, including some in the United States, saw the fulfillment of biblical prophecy.[33] Unfortunately for Christian witness to the Muslim world, these same Christians saw such fulfillment of prophecy as a divine sanction on anything and everything the state of Israel would do thereafter. In essence, these Christians have given Israel a free pass. They support Israel blindly even when it commits brutal and oppressive acts. To add insult to injury, those American Christians with the loudest voices tell the Muslim world that Christians support all types of injustice and brutality committed by Israel against Muslims. Some context is warranted.

After the 1967 war with many of its neighbors, the Israeli military occupied territory outside its legal borders. Palestinian civilians lived in this occupied territory and had for centuries and even millennia. According to international law, after the end of hostilities, Israel was obliged to vacate this territory. It did not do so. The Israeli military remained in these territories, and with the exception of the Gaza Strip, continues to occupy these territories as of this writing. In further violation of international law, Israel began building settlements for Israeli citizens, in some cases bulldozing Palestinian homes and villages in the process. The international community, including the United States, protested the construction of these Israeli settlements on Palestinian land.

In addition, Israel began building highways crisscrossing the Palestinian territory. Israel took control of the water resources in the occupied territories, diverting water away from Palestinian farms and villages and toward the Israeli settlements. Israel gives Palestinians access to running water only a few hours per week, with full service to the Israeli settlements at all other times. Israel created multiple checkpoints throughout the

---

33   For another view, see Gary Burge, *Jesus and the Land: The New Testament Challenge to "Holy Land" Theology* (Grand Rapids: Baker Academic, 2010).

occupied territories, severely restricting movement by Palestinians, and sometimes completely preventing them from traveling to schools, jobs, and medical clinics. Palestinians have given birth and died while tied up at these checkpoints. Israel also blocks delivery of humanitarian aid to the occupied Palestinian territories.

After decades of such treatment, some in the Palestinian community resorted to violence in protest. This included suicide bombings and mortar fire into Israel. These activities are inexcusable and should be condemned. In retaliation, Israel tightened restrictions, imposed twenty-four hour curfews in the occupied territories lasting weeks at a time, and launched military actions to punish the Palestinians. This resulted in thousands of innocent Palestinian deaths.

Israel has a right to exist in peace, a right to defend itself from aggression and violence, and a right to take reasonable precautions to prevent further violence. However, while Israel and a sympathetic media in the West justify *everything* Israel does as defensive, this ignores the underlying illegal occupation by Israel of the Palestinian territory. It also ignores the brutality and oppression with which Israel has treated innocent Palestinians. It is this systematic injustice that draws such ire from Muslims around the world.

Christians must take a more nuanced view and be able to separate support for Israel from support for the unjust and inhumane treatment Israel inflicts on innocent Palestinian civilians. We must condemn injustice and oppression *wherever we find it*. Turning a blind eye to the plight of innocent victims does not reflect godliness, and creates a powerful negative testimony concerning the gospel of Jesus Christ.

When asked why the United States supports Israel so unconditionally, an appropriate answer might be that we cannot speak for the government, but as disciples of Jesus Christ, we support peace for both Israel and the Palestinians, and condemn injustice, oppression, and violence from all parties. Such a response would not only do wonders for the cause of the gospel among Muslims, but also be a much more accurate reflection of the heart of God.

Action Item Checklist

Part 2: Ministering the Gospel to Muslims

☐ Check Your Heart. Does it Reflect God's Love?

☐ Be Proactive in Meeting Muslims
- Frequent places where Muslims congregate
- Use "Salaam" as a greeting

☐ Move Past Superficial Relationships
- Invite them to your home for a meal
- Be vulnerable and share personal struggles

☐ Be a Learner
- Ask questions about their home country and culture
- Ask questions about their family

☐ Determine Their Heart Language
- Arabic, Turkish, Persian, Urdu, English, Malay, Indonesian, Pashto or other

☐ Give Ministry Items as Gifts on Usual Gift-Giving Occasions (ensure it's in their heart language)
- New Testament
- Ministry Movies; "Jesus" Film, "God's Story"

☐ Engage in Spiritual Conversations *as the Holy Spirit Prompts*
- Ask if they have questions about any gifts you've given
- Be confident in sharing your faith or using scripture as you normally would

☐ Be Prepared to Address Theological Objections
- Reliability of the New Testament, Son of God, The Trinity, Sin, The Attributes of God, The Crucifixion, Prophecies of Muhammad, The Gospel of Barnabas, Western Culture and Christianity, Western Support of Israel

☐ Lead Muslims to Faith in Christ!
- "If you confess with your mouth that Jesus is Lord and believe in your heart that God raised him from the dead, you will be saved." Romans 10:9 NLT

CONCLUSION

OVER THE LAST FEW decades, Jesus has appeared to countless Muslims in the form of dreams and waking visions. This phenomenon is very widespread. No one knows how often this has happened, but anecdotally, it is fair to conclude that tens of thousands of Muslims from every corner of the globe have had these supernatural encounters with Jesus. Books and movies relate the testimonies of some of these Muslims. Most often, Muslims who experience these dreams and visions have no prior exposure to Christianity or the Bible. Nothing in their daily experience triggers these dreams. Undoubtedly, this is a movement of the Holy Spirit unlike anything the church has seen since the first century. Whatever the significance of the timing of this phenomenon, one thing is clear. Jesus is drawing Muslims to Himself.

While this is cause for celebration, it is also cause for alarm. Dreams and visions alone do not lead Muslims to saving faith in Jesus. Muslims who have these encounters with Jesus are ready to hear the gospel, to study the New Testament, and to place their faith in Jesus once they understand the gospel. Christians must be ready to assist these fervent seekers and guide them into a saving relationship with Jesus. Treating Muslims with suspicion, or as "the enemy," or in any way other than the way Jesus would treat them, hinders this work of God, and creates a barrier between Muslims and saving faith.

Even apart from dreams and visions, many Muslims know instinctively that, as one Iranian put it, "something is wrong with Islam." The tragedy is that most Muslims know of no other way and have been paralyzed by fear. They fear the sin of questioning God or the sin of questioning Islam. They also fear being ostracized by their families and communities should they divulge their doubts. These Muslims are all around us, some even hoping for a safe, secure and intimate relationship with a Christian so they can air their questions and doubts.

The h can no longer ignore the Muslim world around it. Jesus has commanded our action. The Holy Spirit is stirring. Muslims are seeking.

How will you respond?

GLOSSARY

Ansar – The helpers. These were citizens of Medina that welcomed the Muslims who migrated there from Mecca. They housed the migrants in their homes, fed them, and provided for them.

Baraka – Blessing. Many Muslims throughout the world seek blessings through superstitious ritual practices.

Bida – Innovation. Salafis accuse modern, moderate Muslims of innovation, or mixing foreign ideas with pure Islam.

Caravanserai – An ancient motel for those travelling in caravans.

Caliph – Successor to Muhammad. Leader of Muslims.

Caliphate – The territory ruled by a Caliph.

Daif – A weak hadith.

Ebionites – A heretical Christian sect present in Mecca during Muhammad's time. The Ebionites no longer exist, and are known only through writings of church fathers critical of them. They accepted only the apocryphal Gospel of the Hebrews, which taught that Mary was the Holy Spirit, that Jesus was only a man, and that Jesus was not crucified. Evidence of Ebionite beliefs are present in the Qur'an.

Fatiha – The first sura of the Qur'an. The Fatiha is not included in several early and prominent versions of the Qur'an. Scholars suggest these versions excluded the Fatiha because it is evidently human speech rather than revealed text.

Fatwa – A legal judgment.

Hadd – Limit. The term refers to the specific crimes and penalties described in the Qur'an, which penalties are barbaric to civilized societies. These penalties include amputations, beheadings and whippings.

Hadith – Accounts of the words and deeds of Muhammad.

Hajj – The journey to Mecca to perform an elaborate list of prescribed rituals. The hajj is one of the five pillars of Islam and required of every capable adult Muslim once in their lives.

Halal – Allowed. This term usually refers to meats from particular animals which have been butchered in the Islamically-approved way, and which Muslims are allowed to eat.

Hanif – A pre-Islamic Arab monotheist

Haram – Prohibited. The opposite of halal, the term usually refers to meats prohibited to Muslims, but also refers to other foods and behaviors.

Hasan – A good hadith.

Hijra – The migration of Muhammad and his followers from Mecca to Medina. It is from the date of the hijra, AD 622, that the Islamic era begins. It is also from this date that the Islamic calendar begins.

Ijma – Consensus. This is one of the sources of Islamic law.

Ijtihad – Independent legal reasoning. This is the process undertaking by an authorized Islamic legal authority to determine what the rule of law should be when it is not obvious from the Qur'an or hadith.

Isnad – Chain of transmission. The term refers to the chain of people who repeated to others accounts of what Muhammad said or did, from the first person to see or hear the event or statement, down to the time of the person examining the chain.

Jihad – Struggle. Used for a holy war, or violence in the cause of Islam.

Jinn – In Islam, these are spiritual beings somewhat lower in power than angels and demons, but which are also good, bad or neutral.

Jizya – The tax imposed on Christians and Jews living in Muslim-dominated territories. The tax is designed to humiliate those who pay it, continually reminding them of their second-class status.

Kabah – Literally, "cube." The term refers to the cubical structure, draped in black fabric, in Mecca. It is in the direction of the Kabah that Muslims face when performing the ritual prayers, and to the Kabah that they travel when performing the hajj. Muslims believe the Kabah was originally built by Adam at the precise center of the earth, and was later rebuilt by Abraham and Ishmael.

Majnun – One who is possessed by, or influenced by, jinn.

Mawdu – A false hadith.

Muhajirun – The term referring to those who migrated from Mecca to Medina with Muhammad. They are afforded an especially high status in Islam due to their early conversion.

Qibla – A marker that indicates the direction a Muslim must face when praying in order to be facing the Kabah. It also means the direction itself as opposed to that which marks the direction.

Qur'an – Literally, "recitation." The Qur'an is the book in which the recitations of Muhammad of the words revealed to him by Gabriel are recorded. It is the holy book of Islam.

Rakat – A repetition of particular words and body movements that constitute one unit of ritual prayer

Ramadan – The Islamic calendar month during which Muslims are commanded to carry out the ritual fast

Sadd al-dhara'i – Blocking the means. In Islamic law, the terms refers to things which are legal and permissible in themselves, but are prohibited because they constitute necessary steps along the way to prohibited conduct. A common example is selling grapes to a person known to make wine.

Sahih – Approved, authoritative. The term refers to a hadith that passes muster in terms of both its chain of transmission and content.

Salafi – A person who advocates purifying Islam by returning to the Islam practiced by the "righteous ancestors," or those Muslims of the first three generations of Islam.

Salaam – Peace. The most common Islamic greeting

Salat – The Islamic ritual prayer

Shahada – The Islamic confession of faith. It is "there is no god but Allah, and Muhammad is the Messenger of Allah."

Shari'a – Islamic law

Sura – The word for "chapter" in the Qur'an

Wudu – Ritual washing which must be performed in a specific way prior to performing the ritual prayer and other required rituals in order to obtain ceremonial cleanliness. Ceremonial cleanliness is a necessary prerequisite to Allah accepting the ritual performance and awarding spiritual merit to the worshipper.

Contact Information

REDEMPTION
PRESS

To order additional copies of this book, please visit
www.redemption-press.com.
Also available on Amazon.com and BarnesandNoble.com
Or by calling toll free 1-844-2REDEEM.

For information about The Christian Institute of Islamic Studies,
or for a study guide for this book, please visit tciis.org

CPSIA information can be obtained
at www.ICGtesting.com
Printed in the USA
FFOW05n1513200217

9 781632 328007